time to
write to
yourself

Dedication

To those who have made my path through life more difficult than it needed to have been, thank you. Without you this book would never have been written and I would never have developed the strength of character I needed not only to survive life but to positively thrive.

To those permanent threads in my life, sometimes at the front of my tapestry and sometimes on the reverse, but always part of the weave, I thank you from the depths of my soul. And if, inadvertently, I have caused you bad times along the way, I apologise.

My grateful thanks to Wendy Hobson, Kay Macmullan and Emma Buckley of Foulsham for guiding me through the publication process.

time to
write to
yourself

a guide to journaling for **emotional**
health and **self-development**

dianne sandland

foulsham
LONDON • NEW YORK • TORONTO • SYDNEY

foulsham

The Publishing House, Bennetts Close, Cippenham,
Slough, Berkshire, SL1 5AP, England

Foulsham books can be found in all good bookshops and direct from
www.foulsham.com

ISBN: 978-0-572-03311-8

Cover photograph © Superstock

A CIP record for this book is available from the British Library

Neither the editors of W. Foulsham and Co. Ltd nor the
author nor the publisher take responsibility for any
possible consequences from any treatment, procedure, test,
exercise, action or application of medication or preparation
by any person reading or following the information in this
book. The publication of this book does not constitute the
practice of medicine, and this book does not attempt to
replace any diet or instructions from your doctor. The
author and publisher advise the reader to check with a
doctor before administering any medication or
undertaking any course of treatment or exercise.

Printed in Great Britain by Creative Print & Design (Wales), Ebbw Vale

Contents

	How to Use this Book	7
Chapter 1	Introduction to Journaling	9
Chapter 2	Therapeutic Writing	13
Chapter 3	Talking Therapies	16
Chapter 4	The Writer's Journaling Experience	21
Chapter 5	A Brief History of Journaling	23
Chapter 6	Skills and Equipment	28
Chapter 7	Poetry for the Terrified	33
Chapter 8	What is Healing?	38
	Loss, Change and Grief	43
Chapter 9	Bereavement	45
Chapter 10	The Death of a Child	54
Chapter 11	Losing a Child when a Relationship Ends	59
Chapter 12	Marriage, Relationships and Divorce	64
Chapter 13	Losing Your Job	73
Chapter 14	Losing a Friend	77
Chapter 15	Losing Your Health	82

	Emotional Health and Healing	89
Chapter 16	Depression	93
Chapter 17	Addictions	98
Chapter 18	Recovering from Childhood Abuse	105
Chapter 19	Eating Disorders	112
Chapter 20	Stress	116
Chapter 21	Anger Management	124
	Physical Health	129
Chapter 22	Keeping a Wellness Journal	130
Chapter 23	Auto-immune Diseases	132
Chapter 24	Dealing with Terminal Illness	136
Chapter 25	Healing through Humour	140
	Other Benefits of Journaling	143
Chapter 26	Personal Growth	145
Chapter 27	Self-esteem	150
Chapter 28	Self-image	154
Chapter 29	Work and Career Motivation	158
Chapter 30	Goal, Reality, Options, Will	163
	Afterword	165
	Resources	167
	Useful Information	183
	Helplines	184
	Bibliography	186
	Index	190

How to Use this Book

Writing a journal can help you to understand the past, deal with the present and look forward positively to the future. This book is designed to help you learn some of the techniques of journal writing and thus work towards changing your life for the better.

I didn't write this book in the order it is presented here and you don't need to read it in that order either – although you can if you wish; you are, after all, the master of your own destiny, an idea that is the crux of many of the exercises you will find within these pages. Each of the chapters can stand alone, so if a particular issue resonates with you, then I suggest you go straight to that part of the book and start working on the relevant exercises.

Many of the exercises are based on two of the so-called 'talking therapies': Cognitive Behaviour Therapy (CBT) and Rational Emotive Behaviour Therapy (REBT). It is this combination of therapeutic journaling, CBT and REBT that makes this book different from others that you may find on the subject.

Rather than repeat myself in every chapter, I have included chapters on therapeutic writing (see page 13) and talking therapies (see page 16) in which I explain how these underpin the exercises. By understanding the basics of the talking therapies, in particular, you could devise your own writing exercises specific to the situation in which you find yourself. In this way, the information you find in this book can be adapted to any situation.

If you are new to keeping a journal, see Chapter 6 (page 28), which explains what you need, why you need it and where to get it. Basically, though, if you've got a pen and paper to hand, you can start right now.

In the Resources section at the back of the book, you will find templates for the journaling processes most often used in the exercises. You can photocopy these templates, write on them directly and then stick them in your journal (you'll need to enlarge them to give yourself enough space for writing if you choose to do this) or if you prefer, you can refer to them as prompts when you are writing in your journal. My preference would be for the second method so that you are not imposing limits on how much you write under each heading.

Finally, you will find that in some places I have used 'he' whilst, in others, I have used 'she'. These are all interchangeable. I was very conscious that I didn't want to direct the book at one gender in particular. Journaling works for everybody.

1 *Introduction to Journaling*

Stillbirth, child abuse and raising an autistic child; none of these subjects were part of my original concept for this book. In my imagination I saw a simple and elegant how-to book based on clinical evidence with occasional reference to my personal experience of the therapeutic value of journaling. Yet, as I wrote, I discovered that I know only one way of teaching and that is the method I use in my day-to-day life when involved in teaching student midwives; I use my experiences, both good and bad, to illustrate the point I'm trying to get across. What this means is that, peppered throughout this book, you will find references to events from my own life. I have tried to keep these to a minimum – who knows, someday somebody might invite me to write my autobiography!

Realising that I would be involved in a certain amount of disclosure wasn't the only thing that transformed my initial perception of what the finished book would be. As I delved more deeply into the healing properties of journaling I became aware that what I had naturally been doing when I wrote in my journals bore a very strong resemblance to some of the 'talking therapies'. So, rather than write just the straightforward book about journaling that I had envisaged, I ended up combining accepted psychological theories with my own experience to create the exercises you will find at the end of each chapter. I believe that in doing this I have produced something new, and different to other books about therapeutic writing.

Why write things down? I'm sure you've found, just as I have, that when you turn things over and over in your mind all that results is confusion and an immersion in the original problem from which it is difficult to swim free. Many therapies rely on talking and, in the best case scenario, that talking will be with somebody who is able to mirror back your innermost thoughts to help you make some sense out of them. When you engage in the style of journaling that I advocate in this book, you will be replacing the counsellor of traditional therapy with the pages of your journal. Essentially, in therapeutic writing, your counsellor is available to you 24 hours a day for 365 days a year – all in the comfort of your own home!

With traditional counselling, unless 'homework' is done conscientiously, the only action required from the client is to turn up to the appointment. On the face of it, this should not be too difficult but, when you are in the depths of despair, it can seem like a major undertaking, and to leave the house and turn up for a clinic appointment may well feel like a step too far. Having suffered from clinical depression, I know that action sometimes feels almost impossible and that the simple task of getting the book and pen from another room may seem too much to ask. It is much simpler, however, than getting the bus or driving to your therapist. You can write in your journal without even having to get washed and dressed.

Expressive Arts Therapy

During my research I discovered a diverse branch of therapies that come under the umbrella of 'healing through action'. As an alternative to being talked at, medicated or analysed, these therapies involve the patient or client in doing things to help get in touch with deep inner issues that might be causing emotional distress. One of these therapies that I found of particular interest was Expressive Arts Therapy (EAT).

It is generally accepted that a child's state of mind can be judged by the artwork he or she produces. Surely, then, if artwork represents the inner feelings so well, it can also be used to modify those inner feelings and, diagnostically, to measure progress in healing. In addition to the drawing and painting that most of us imagine to be art, EAT encompasses a whole line-up of creative pursuits, such as music, drama, play, dance, guided imagery, poetry, creative writing and journaling: something to suit almost everybody.

As I am tone deaf and have no natural sense of rhythm, to attempt to express myself through music and dance would simply make me feel inadequate. On the other hand, I love the written word and take great delight in finding just the right expression for a given circumstance; so creative writing and journaling are perfect for me. And since any work I do in this discipline is between me and myself, I can even try poetry because nobody is going to know if the results are pure twaddle. And, just maybe, the discipline involved in capturing an emotion or thought in a few well-chosen words will help to distil my sense of what is going on in my life.

So, if you would be more comfortable giving a name to the type of journaling discussed in this book, I suppose we could call it Expressive Arts Therapy. I think, however, that the added components from the talking therapies mean that it's EAT with something extra.

Rational Emotive Behaviour Therapy

While researching for this book I also came across a therapy known as Rational Emotive Behaviour Therapy (REBT), a branch of Cognitive Behaviour Therapy (CBT). It was in these ideas that I was astounded to find the theory behind what I have been doing in my journals for years. I may not have undertaken my work with REBT in any structured or formal way, in fact compared to the science, my use of the principles were very naive. Nevertheless, there is no doubt that REBT is what I have been doing.

The basis of this therapy is that people can only change their attitudes and their lives by changing their thought processes. This is so fundamental to the beliefs underpinning this book that I have included a chapter explaining CBT and REBT and the underlying principles (see Chapter 3, page 16), in the hope that it will help to explain how I have formulated some of the exercises in this book. More importantly, perhaps, with this basic understanding you will be able to formulate your own journaling exercises, specific to your own situation.

I must make it clear here that I am not qualified in any of the psychotherapeutic sciences, nor am I proposing that this book should be seen as a thesis on any area of that branch of medicine. Simply, I want to demonstrate that, as well as being an enjoyable exercise in its own right, keeping a journal has the potential to heal body, mind and soul.

In fact, it seems that, contrary to popular perception, talking to oneself may not be a sign of imminent madness; in fact, it could be the first step on the path to regaining or preserving your sanity.

2 Therapeutic Writing

Psychologists have long been aware that the outward expression of feelings brings about benefits for our mental health, but it is only in the past two or three decades that scientists have realised that journaling can potentially make a positive impact on our physical health. The realisation of this potential has resulted in a crop of research studies dating from the 1980s, each of which explores the health benefits of expressive writing.

We know that journal writing results in psychological benefits for healthy people, such as stress reduction and the opportunity to self-counsel, whether that involves exploring dreams or disentangling the adult mind from negative childhood experiences. What is even more exciting is that researchers have started to prove that journaling also benefits people with physical illness. In fact, over the last ten or so years there have been several studies set up to investigate the therapeutic effect of writing.

Results of research studies

One study, undertaken in the USA showed that 47 per cent of patients with rheumatoid arthritis or asthma, both chronic conditions, experienced an improvement in their symptoms after they had written about the most traumatic event in their lives. In the control group, who wrote about everyday topics, the improvement rate was 24 per cent, which I still find astounding. The other interesting point raised by this study is that it is what you write and how you write it that influences whether the exercise will be therapeutic. After all, if all writing were healing then we'd feel better for writing a shopping list!

In the most well known study, undertaken by Professor Pennebaker of Austin University in Texas, participants were asked to write for a period of 15 minutes every day for four days. They were encouraged to 'really let go of [their] very deepest emotions and thoughts'. The health of the participants was monitored following this, and comparisons were made to their health status prior to the writing experiment. The results were conclusive – those who had written about their thoughts and feelings had significantly reduced their visits to the doctor. And it wasn't just the reduction in visits to the doctor that was noteworthy; several markers of physical health found in blood samples were also changed. Perhaps the most important one being an increase in T-cell production, a result of increased immunity.

Yet other studies have demonstrated that writing about personal trauma is related to a decrease in pain and reduced use of pain-killing medication. The underpinning theory behind all of this is that by writing down and subsequently making sense of negative things that have happened in your life, you are able to consign these events to history. In effect, they become part of your past rather than hanging around in your brain and remaining part of your present. Interestingly, there is a suggestion that men might benefit even more than women from undertaking writing exercises, although this theory requires further investigation before it can be substantiated.

Benefits of journaling

Writing in a journal is like having a friend you can trust implicitly not to betray your confidences. In the safety of its pages you can begin to discover your dreams and fantasies, confront your fears, and learn to understand your belief system and where it came from. Not only can you trust your diary more than any other human being, you can also rely on it to be there whenever you want for however long you want; you can express your anger, your hurt and your pain and know that, no matter what you say or how clumsily you express yourself, your diary will still be there next time you need it.

The secret is to write to yourself, and for yourself, because if you write with the belief that your words are for publication or that somebody else is going to read them, you will censor your thoughts and the words you write without even realising that you are doing so. Your diary is for you and you alone. It is the friend who won't throw a wobbly because you haven't called in ages; it will never get bored with you when you write things over and over again in an attempt to get a handle on them. When you write vitriol about your mother-in-law it won't tell on you; when you write your goals and ambitions it won't laugh at you. It will simply act as a mirror, reflecting back to you all that you are and all that you could be.

The purpose of this book is to share and explore with you the therapeutic qualities of honouring your thoughts, fears, loves and desires by making them real, that is, by writing them down. It's not always an easy journey but it is a remarkable one. I would be honoured to be your companion and guide.

3 Talking Therapies

Talking therapies are exactly what they say they are – you talk and somebody listens. The principle behind them is that as you talk you release tension and are able to express previously unspoken thoughts and feelings and, in doing so, have the opportunity to explore the feelings and move on.

Research into these therapies highlights the fact that most people welcome the opportunity to discuss their innermost thoughts. The same research also points out that many people have definite requirements from these therapies, the main ones being: the need to be believed and accepted, the need to feel safe, and the need not to be judged. Interviews with therapy-service users, undertaken by Alison Faulkner in 1997 as part of the 'Knowing our own minds' project, show that two groups of people who stand out as having found talking therapies particularly useful were survivors of sexual abuse and Asian women. The same survey showed that access to these services for these groups was noted as being problematic.

So, we know that exploring your feelings works, but we also know that there can be problems both in delivering the service and in accessing the service. Given the declared problems with accessing the service, could the results of the survey have been skewed, with only those in desperate need being able to jump through the necessary hoops in order to get help and therefore being the only ones to take part in the research? My reason for posing this question is a belief that it is not just the two groups identified who would benefit from an exploration of their inner feelings. I believe the majority of people have something to gain from understanding how their thought processes work.

Given the results of this research, I would argue that journaling is an excellent substitute for the talking therapies and, in some cases, infinitely better. Your journal is always available, it will not judge you, it is private and safe and it will accept whatever you write in it without argument. What it will do is reflect back what you have written so that, once again in safety and without judgement, you can dispute your own negative thought processes and replace them with something far more positive. And that is the basis of both Rational Emotive Behaviour Therapy (REBT) and Cognitive Behaviour Therapy (CBT), both of which are very briefly explained below.

Cognitive Behaviour Therapy and Rational Emotive Behaviour Therapy

Cognition means 'to know', so this is a therapy about getting a client to know himself and his thought processes. The 'behaviour' part of the title refers to the ways people behave when they are depressed or in emotional pain. These behaviours can compound the original problem and lengthen the time it takes to become well again.

The aim of CBT is to assist the client to understand the relationship between thoughts, feelings and behaviour. During discussions, the therapist and the client will attempt to reach an agreement about the nature of the current problem in the client's life. Based on this shared view of the issues, a strategy will be drawn up that enables the client to specify certain goals and objectives.

Following the agreement of realistic goals and objectives, the main focus of this therapy will be on teaching the client to isolate the initial thought in a negative thought spiral, and on acquiring the practical skills needed to break that spiral of negative thought. By using this new insight, the client will be enabled to achieve his set goals, allowing him the satisfaction of knowing that improvements in his pattern of thought and, therefore, in his behaviour have been achieved by his own efforts.

REBT comes under the general heading of CBT with the major difference being that it accepts that, due to biological reasons, not everybody will be able to modify their thought patterns to the same degree. Rational, in the sense it is used here, means realistic, and REBT asks us to understand that some negative thoughts are unavoidable and, in some cases, actually helpful. For example, nobody expects you to think positively when somebody close to you has just died. Apart from anything else, to do so would interfere with the mourning process.

The founder of REBT, Dr Ellis, tells us that this therapy is not about positive thinking but about realistic thinking. It also takes as its premise the idea that a person's belief system is a product of both biology and ways of thinking that have been acquired over many years. From the biological perspective, some people have an inherited pre-disposition to depression, anger, psychosis and a whole range of emotional disturbances, and these tendencies will limit how far a person can change his thinking patterns. In terms of the ways of thinking that we acquire during a lifetime, REBT works on the premise that it is not the traumas of our childhood that cause our emotional pain but the negative thought processes we have built up surrounding those traumas.

REBT is based on a theory of causation: our emotions and our behaviours are the result of the way we think. When I talk about the way we think, I am referring to how we think about everything – the world, other people, ourselves, our jobs, our homes and our families. If you are a person who is prone to depression, your thought processes will be skewed and you will misinterpret things that happen in your life; you will look at events with your 'depression glasses' on; you will see things as being gloomier than they really are.

For instance, if somebody at work has pointed out a minor error in something you have done, rather than thinking that you have been given the opportunity to correct the error before it goes any further, you may think 'I'm useless at my job, I always knew it. Now everybody will know how useless I am.' In the cold light of day we can all look at that belief and see how irrational it is, but I, for one, am guilty of that exact thought process – that's why I chose it as an example – and the simple law of averages says that many more hundreds if not thousands of people have travelled the same route.

REBT encourages you to accept yourself as you really are, in my case somebody who is prone to depression, whilst at the same time giving you tools that will help you to develop new ways of thinking. The knock-on effect is acquisition of a long-term skill to aid rational thinking.

The application of CBT and REBT to journaling

By examining and changing my thought processes through my writing I have long been using the ideas behind CBT and REBT. I was excited to discover, however, that these positive changes can be achieved yet more effectively by applying the REBT technique for thought adaptation to journaling. And it really is as simple as ABC:

* **A** The **activating event** is whatever happened to start the irrational thought process.

* **B** Your **beliefs** are behind your tendency to think irrationally about what happened.

* **C** The **consequence** is the way that you are feeling (angry, depressed, etc.) and is due to a combination of the activating event and your beliefs.

* **D** You now need to **dispute** the beliefs that underpin your reactions

* **E** and replace the disputed old belief with an **effective** new belief and, therefore, a new **emotional** consequence.

What I had been doing for decades, without the benefit of this framework, was to examine and dispute my beliefs within the pages of my journals. I now believe that by using the REBT technique when you write you will be able to harness the already well-known healing potential of writing and make it work even harder for you. And that, I believe, is what makes this book different from others you may find on journaling – it takes an accepted and substantiated therapeutic technique and adapts it so that anybody can access it. And you can use it in the privacy of your own home at whatever time of day or night suits you.

Not all of the exercises in the book are based on REBT techniques, but a great many of them are. In the Resources section (see page 168) you will find a template for using the ABC technique. I suggest that you photocopy this and keep it in your journal as an aide-memoire. Alternatively, you could photocopy a supply of these templates to write on. However, you may find that the space limitation this imposes and the fact that you will be left with a loose sheet of paper that could get mislaid or misappropriated, limits you from examining your thoughts as deeply as you would if you were to write in your journal.

4 The Writer's Journaling Experience

Like many of you, I expect, when I was a teenager I kept a diary. My particular version was the ubiquitous 1970s red plastic-trying-to-be-leather variant, complete with brass lock and key. That poor, insubstantial book chronicled my teenage loves, fears and sexual experiments, until one day somebody I trusted broke into it and violated my privacy. The lack of key did not cause the intruder a problem; he simply used kitchen scissors to cut the plastic strap. I no longer have that diary. It was defiled by the trespasser and it became a source of anguish rather than solace. So, at that point, diaries and I parted company and, such is my aversion to them, I even have problems keeping my appointments diary up to date.

In 1993 I began a three-year period of training to become a midwife. To my horror, in addition to all the required academic work and the longed-for clinical placements, I was instructed to keep a reflection diary, an obligation I viewed with something akin to horror although, initially, I paid lip service to it. Not only could I not see any reason for this added task, I couldn't see where on earth I was going to find the time.

As a mature student with two small boys and a husband who was vehemently opposed to my entry into anything to do with the National Health Service, I was already batting from a sticky wicket. My life was a constant round of juggling various responsibilities in an attempt to run my home life as if midwifery didn't exist; as the course was full time and included shift-work it was, I have to say, a vain attempt. My husband's opposition to the course caused many problems over the three years – emotional as well as practical – and, because I felt it would negatively impact on my carefully crafted 'strong woman' persona to admit that I was struggling,

I increasingly found solace in the reflection diary. Whether that was its intended purpose, I have no idea, but it proved to be a steadfast friend in times of emotional need.

Then, in the summer of 1995, life dropped a bombshell on me from a great height. My mother was diagnosed with terminal cancer and given three weeks to live. My worst fear, the one that had haunted me since childhood, was coming true. My mother took to her bed and waited for the inevitable and, in my desperate need to experience every available moment in her company, I put my life on hold and took to bed with her. The three weeks stretched into five months, during which time I saw indignities and pain I could barely comprehend. From a joyously funny woman I watched my mother degenerate by increments to a frail woman trapped by an unfaithful body. Simply by looking into her eyes, I knew her intellect was still alive, but that dreadful invader of her body had taken away all means of communication. During that frightening and painful autumn and winter my journal became a crucible for my soul.

Now in my fifties and recently diagnosed with a chronic and very painful disease, I once again find solace in talking to myself through the pages of a journal. I don't write every day, although I think about writing every day. The thinking is nowhere near as therapeutic as the doing; in fact, I would go as far as to say it is completely counterproductive. Whereas writing it all down brings a great relief from the gloom and despondency that threatens to envelop me, simply thinking about the issues seems to deepen that gloom. Brooding, I suppose.

5 *A Brief History of Journaling*

It is no surprise, I suppose, that the main contributors to the world of journaling of the type we discuss in this book have been women. Of course, there is an illustrious history of male diary writers – Samuel Pepys and Daniel Defoe, for instance – but men tend to document facts rather than explore their innermost thoughts and feelings. So, whilst their words tend to give us a valuable and accurate account of the place and time they inhabited, there is very little sense of the diary as a repository of personal reflection.

Sappho

One of the earliest female chroniclers, who shares her views of the world with us, is Sappho. Although most people relate her name to lesbianism, due to the fact that she lived on the isle of Lesbos as part of a female commune, she was, in fact, married and had at least one child. Her preferred form of reflecting on life was the song, in which she took an unflinching look at the lives of her compatriots and herself. It seems she had her tongue firmly in her cheek and was, maybe, one of the first female satirists. She was also remarkably adept at capturing bodily sensations, as illustrated in the following excerpt from her 'Hymn to Aphrodite'.

'and cold sweat holds me and shaking

grips me all, greener than grass

I am and dead – or almost

I seem to me'

Pillow books

Travelling further east, and moving forward in time by about 1500 years, we come to pillow books, a form of journaling undertaken by Japanese ladies at court. In these books they would record memories, imaginings and gossip. One of the most readable was kept by Sei Shonagon, an assistant to the Empress Sadako in 990 CE. The following excerpt shows how down to earth her diaries are and demonstrates how some thoughts and feelings are universal:

> 'When I first went into waiting at Her Majesty's Court, so many different things embarrassed me that I could not even reckon them up and I was always on the verge of tears. As a result, I tried to avoid appearing before the Empress except at night, and even then I stayed behind a three-foot curtain of state.'

Simple and from the heart, I can almost feel her blushes and imagine her contrivances to be seen only at night. The name 'Shonagon' translates as 'minor counsellor', so we can assume that in terms of influence and importance she ranked very low in the court, helping us to understand her feelings of embarrassment and unworthiness. Her writings correspond closely to the type of journaling I am advocating within this book, as can be seen in her introduction:

> 'Everything that I have seen and felt is included.'

European diarists

Moving forward in time again, this time to Europe in the middle of the second century CE, we find Leonor Lopez's description of her imprisonment in Seville and the subsequent 20 years of her life. Although, on the surface, her memoirs describe her religious beliefs, they also describe her repatriation from poverty to wealth and status, as an advisor to Queen Catalina. Her writings are a tribute to female strength and an example of feminine guile.

At around the same time and still in Europe, we find Italian Teresa de Cartagena, granddaughter of Salomon Ha-Levi, a former rabbi. Salomon converted to the Christian faith, eventually holding the title Bishop of Cartagena. When Teresa was a young girl, she was afflicted with profound deafness as a result of an illness. She eventually took holy orders and became a nun and it was during this time that she wrote her diaries. Surprisingly, her writings do not speak of her religious beliefs, but document her inner struggle to come to terms with her infirmity, just as I advocate in this book. It seems that nothing is new.

Anne Frank

We can't write a history of diarists, no matter how brief, without including Anne Frank. A Jewish girl born in Germany but living in Holland, Anne was 13 years old when she was given a diary for her birthday. The date was 12 June 1942 and she started writing immediately. I suspect that, like all of us, Anne filled that first sheet of paper with her very best handwriting but that, by the third page or so, as her pen raced across the page trying to keep up with her thoughts, her writing deteriorated.

Her first entries were similar to those in thousands of teenage diaries. She spoke about her friends and family, she described her school life and wrote about the boys she liked to flirt with, and she tells us what she looks like. However, as the oppression of her people worsened, she began to write about wider issues, for instance she talks about the yellow star that all Jews were obliged to wear in public.

A month after Anne started to keep her diary, her sister Margot was called up for relocation to a work camp. The family had heard such horror stories about these camps and were so determined to stay together that they decided to go into hiding. Their bolt-hole was a suite of concealed rooms at Anne's father's workplace, alongside a canal in Amsterdam.

The rest of Anne's diary tells us of the horrors of that time in their secret hideaway and, later on, we learn how she managed to keep emotionally strong in a concentration camp. What makes for such compelling reading is the fact that this is not just a chronicle of events. Anne writes about her emotions and she writes from her heart. We learn of her hopes and her fears, her feelings and her beliefs. To read her diary is to feel as if we are being taken into her confidence; she shares with us things that she could not or would not share with anybody else. She tells us 'when I write, I can shake off all my cares'. Her final entry was made on 1 August 1944. Naked and emaciated, she eventually died whilst in Belsen concentration camp, just a few days after the death of her sister. It was March 1945 and she was apparently the victim of an outbreak of typhus.

Weblogs

To bring this brief history up to date, I can't escape the fact that, in the past decade or so, technology has entered the world of journaling in a big way. The weblog, commonly known as a blog, has exploded on to the scene and shows no sign of going away. As a grumpy old woman and traditionalist, I don't particularly favour this mode of self-expression but, if I look hard enough, I suppose I can see the attractions: no pen or paper needed and, provided you set a password, no fear of your thoughts being plundered by your closest family and friends. Although, of course, publishing your fears and fantasies on the web is no guarantee of privacy!

For me, putting one's innermost thoughts and emotional struggles on the web defeats the object of keeping a journal in the first place. I appreciate the luxury of having a private sanctuary where I can look at my thoughts and put them into some sort of order; a place where I can make sense of the world; a sort of meditation in writing. I do wonder if those who keep their journals in such a public place are privately hoping that their writing will be 'discovered' and either published or turned into a blockbusting movie. Now, there's a journaling topic for you – if your life was made into a movie, who would you choose to play you?

Men and journaling

The diarists I have included here were all chosen because they used their journals as a repository for their deepest thoughts and emotions. Perhaps to keep a journal is a particularly female occupation, whilst men tend to keep factual diaries or accounts. Recent research demonstrates what a huge shame that is. Pennebaker's work (see page 14) has established that it is men who benefit more from examining their feelings between the covers of a journal. It doesn't take a scientist to work out that this is probably because, in general, men don't share their feelings with another as often as women do.

If you have a man in your life that could use some therapy, why not share this book with him? The worst he can do is curl a derisory lip and say 'no', and if, by some chance, he says 'yes', the scientific evidence suggests that he will become a happier and healthier man to live with. As a final thought, who would choose to play *him* in the movie of your life?

6 Skills and Equipment

One of the beauties of journaling is that you don't need any fancy, expensive equipment to get started; all you need is something to write with and something to write on. You are sure to have both of these in the house already, and no special purchases will be required. Then again, for those of us who are passionate about exquisite things, the sky is the limit in terms of what you can spend to heighten the pleasure of the undertaking.

Over the years, I have written my thoughts down on everything from scraps of paper of every hue, Post-it notes and white lined index cards to beautifully hand-tooled leather-bound volumes specially imported from the United States. All have been adequate but it is difficult to assess any personal changes that my writing might have brought about when faced with a box filled with loose scraps of paper and card. On the other hand, who's to say that my expensive products render the writing process any more beneficial?

If, like me, you have a tendency to think that costly means better, please think again. You can more than adequately record your thoughts in a cheap spiral-bound notebook using a ballpoint pen or pencil. However, having made a start and found that the process is, indeed, therapeutic, the chances are that you will want to upgrade the paper on which you write and, once you get to this stage, there are number of points to take into consideration.

Paper size

Frequently I find that I experience something that I would desperately like to write down immediately – either for posterity or because I want to explore the repercussions of the event in greater depth. For this reason, I believe that a portable journal is a good idea. If you purchase one, however, you may find it languishes in your bag unused. The only way to find out if this will be the case is to buy one and see, which is exactly what I did. I will never need to buy a journal of this size again as I found that I am far too self-conscious to whip my little book out in public and start scribbling away. Consequently, for me, something similar to A5 size is best.

A topic that is not really discussed in this book is using art and multi-media in your journal. If you like to express yourself in this way, a bigger journal – perhaps A4 or larger – may be useful.

Paper quality

The question of artwork leads us on to paper quality. If you are going to be using 'wet' media, you will need paper that is strong enough to withstand the wetting and thick enough not to allow your work to bleed through to the other side of the page. The binding is important too because if you are going to be sticking mementoes or other 3D items into your book you will find this easier with a binding that can expand to take the extra volume, such as an art notebook with spiral binding. An alternative to this is to tear out every other page, thereby giving more space for your embellishments. Even without artwork, a spiral-bound book is much nicer to use because it lies completely flat.

I have to admit, however, that the majority of my journals were bought because I fell in love with the cover and gave little thought to what was underneath it. For instance, I have a personal dislike of lined paper as it brings back memories of the cheap blue-lined writing paper of my childhood, yet a number of my journals are lined because I was seduced by the beautiful binding and failed to look inside at the time of purchase. It's important to say, though, that I still use them.

Writing implements

Having sorted out the question of paper, we need to move on to what you are going to write with. Really, as with paper, it is totally down to your own personal choice and budget. However, you may find, as I do, that keeping a special pen for journal-writing lends a sort of ritual atmosphere to the event that, over time, may help to make your writing time even more productive by keeping it separate from, say, writing a letter to the school to explain your child's absence. For your more creative entries there is so much available that you will be spoiled for choice.

Preserving your journal

Perhaps the final point to consider when thinking about your journaling supplies is the longevity of the work you produce. Do you want it to last longer than you do? In an ideal world you would write with archival inks on archival papers and store the completed books in archival conditions. As we all know, this isn't an ideal world, but there are some steps you can take to prolong the life of your journal.

* Try to use archival quality paper, acid-free and 80lb weight or heavier.

* If you want to store items in plastic sleeves, polypropylene, polyethylene and DuPont Mylar™ are archival.

* If you are attaching things like flowers, place them in a polyethylene pocket or bag and stitch it to the page using cotton.

* Photographs and other flat media should be attached with archival photo corners. Whatever you do, don't use sticky tape because it will eventually yellow and may well ooze sticky gunk all over the page, ruining your work in the process.

* When attaching newsprint, fold the top over to produce a hinge and stick this into your book using water-soluble glue or a glue stick.

❋ Most importantly, never laminate. The contents of the laminate pouch will decay along with the plastic.

Writing ability

Having briefly discussed the materials required, I feel I should say something about skill, and I can say what I want to say in just three words – no skill required.

In my experience the reason most frequently given for not writing a journal is that the person cannot write. This never fails to amaze me because, as far as I am concerned, if you can talk, you can write. I am well aware that for a few unfortunate people this doesn't necessarily follow – my own mother was a very fluent reader and speaker but could not write anything more than her own name due to suffering from a form of dyslexia. However, in most circumstances, if you are reading this book then the chances are that you can write. Remember that you are not sitting down to write a philosophical treatise or a great work of literature – you are merely recording your inner voice. Additionally, nobody is ever going to see what you have written unless you make a conscious effort to share your work.

To journal you simply have to sit down, take a deep breath to centre yourself and let the words flow from your pen. And I promise you that they will flow. It is a process that is almost magical; there you sit with pen poised and nothing in particular on your mind when, seemingly from nowhere, out come the words. If you can resist the temptation to worry about grammar and spelling, and if you forget about trying to achieve a certain style in your writing, you will find that the words continue to flow. They might well start as a tiny trickle but eventually you will find yourself paddling in a stream of them, each idea begetting another until, eventually you will find yourself totally and blissfully immersed in what you are writing. What is more, those words will be your own unique voice – no attempt at style required.

When, for whatever reason, the words do dry up, look to the exercises, ideas and prompts in this book to get those journalistic juices flowing once more. If you find that meditating helps to de-clutter the mind in preparation for writing, you may choose to use the instructions for a simple meditation in the Resources section (see page 170). And if the suggestion to try writing poetry seems a step too far, then look to the following chapter for some ideas that make this a much more approachable method.

7 Poetry for the Terrified

You will see that in a number of the chapters I suggest that you try your hand at poetry, an idea that will have many of you running for the hills. The reality is that there is absolutely no reason for the disquiet many of us feel when attempting to read or write poetry. In a way, writing poetry is a bit like writing music and perhaps that's why many of us are scared to try. It is rhythm that distinguishes poetry from prose, and which leads us to associate it more with writing music than writing words, but rhythm can be as simple or as complicated as you wish to make it.

A superb book to get hold of if you are thinking of writing more than the occasional poem is *The Ode Less Travelled* by Stephen Fry. With his usual intelligent good humour, he completely demystifies the process of poetry and explains techniques such as metre, rhyme and form in an understandable way. For the purposes of journaling though, there is no need to go out and buy a book on the subject. For one thing, only you will ever see your attempts and, for another, once you lose your fear of rhythm and start to play with the words, you will find that you not only enjoy the process but also turn out passable work.

In this chapter I give you suggestions and examples of simple forms of poetry and some techniques for helping you to forget that you're writing poetry while you concentrate on the words. If you don't enjoy the process, there is no need to continue; journaling is supposed to be therapeutic and not cause you additional stress as you struggle with something you are not enjoying. But do have a go – you have nothing to lose and you might find you enjoy it.

Bantu

Named after the Bantu tribe of Africa, this style of poetry relies on the power of metaphor. Bantu verse consists of two lines; the first line is an observation and the second line replies with a metaphor. For instance:

The television is on in the bedroom

While the moon is on in the sky.

Or

My husband walked out of my life

Like a boat sailing out of its harbour.

Alphabet

I really like this one and used it for the poem about how angry I was when my mother died (see page 47), although you wouldn't realise it when you read it now. What this simple process does is make you think so hard about how to use the next letter of the alphabet that you forget you are writing poetry. When you have written all 26 lines, you have the bones of a poem that you can then flesh out. I've written the following two verses as an example:

Alison stopped and Alison looked

Behind her, to see if he had ever really

Cared about her or if he was simply being

Dutiful in staying with her.

Ethan stopped and Ethan looked

For Alison, to see if she had ever really

Given herself to him, or if she was simply

Holding on to her past.

Lists

Choose a phrase that says what it is you want to say, for example, 'I want', 'I love', 'I miss', 'I need', 'I call'. Start each line of your poem with this phrase, simply stating what it is, for example, you need:

I need wholeness

I need to belong

I need you

I need to come home.

I need to come home

I need you

I need to belong

I need wholeness.

The five senses

Describe something or somebody using the five senses. For instance, the following on an ended love affair:

I saw your familiar face as you came through the door and

I smelled the leather of your jacket as I kissed that countenance.

I heard the creak of that jacket as you let it drop, then

I smelled your skin as you stroked my hair. Now,

I taste your tang as I explore your remains with my mind.

The 5 Ws

Write a five-line poem answering the questions: who?, what?, when?, where?, why? Try rewriting the verse above using the 5 Ws.

35

Who (or what) is the subject of the poem?

What are they doing?

When are they doing it?

Where are they doing it?

Why are they doing it?

Rhythm

Nursery rhymes have a very simple but obvious rhythm, which is ideal for basing your poetry on. The rhythm of 'Mary had a Little Lamb', for example, is:

didum didum didum didum

didum didum didum

didum didum didum didum

didum didum didum

One of my favourites is 'Star Light, Star Bright'. It took me quite a while to dissect the rhythm of this one and I'm still not sure that I've got it right. What do you think?

didum, didum

didum didum didum

didum didum, didum didum

didum didum didum didum

Feelings as metaphor

Choose the feeling you want to write about. Now think about how you might describe that feeling using metaphor. What about anger as a dark red gemstone or love as a marshmallow; jealousy as a green snake or joy as a crystal fountain?

Haiku

This form of Japanese poetry is made up of three lines and 17 syllables in the following pattern:

Line one: 5 syllables

Line two: 7 syllables

Line three: 5 syllables

As Haiku is usually used for poetry about nature, it would be an ideal form to use if you want to describe a place of beauty that you shared with somebody you love.

Using poetry

The thing with poetry is that it cuts away all the dross and leaves you with a distillation of the emotions you want to express. A well-crafted poem can say more than a thousand words. And if, like mine, your poems are less than well-crafted, just remember that the time you have taken trying to express your feelings in this way has also been time spent examining these feelings. So whatever the quality of your ode, the outcome will be the same: a greater understanding of your feelings. And nobody will ever see your poems unless, of course, you choose to publish them.

Please do give it a go. You will find that it's more fun than you think and it can be quite addictive.

8 What is Healing?

Having looked at journaling in terms of how it can help, how it has been done in the past and how you too can start to tap into its advantages, it makes sense to consider in more detail what it is we want to gain from journaling. I believe that journaling can bring healing to all areas of our life. We hear the word 'healing' so often, though, that it has become part of the pattern on the wallpaper. My intention was to start this section with a dictionary definition of the word 'healing' but, the more I thought about it, the less I liked the idea.

It is not dictionary definitions that are important in the context of this book or this chapter; it is what the word 'healing' means to you that is paramount. Does it make you think of doctors, faith healers, spiritual healers? Maybe it brings to mind herbalists and homeopaths. If we are to travel this road together it is vital that we are both heading towards the same point on the map. If you think we're going to Bali, your expectations will be quite different to those you would have if you think we're going to Birmingham!

The limitations of medicine

As a health professional I am conversant with the science of medicine; I've seen miracles wrought by highly trained and skilled people and I have a genuine and deep respect for my professional colleagues. As a midwife, I understand the science of the female body and, as part of my work, I have been responsible for stemming a major haemorrhage from a mother following the birth of her child. I know, for instance, that if the bladder is full the uterus cannot contract efficiently, which can result in dramatic and life-threatening blood loss following childbirth. I know which drugs to use and how to use them to override the body's malfunction and cause the uterus to contract, whether it wants to or not. But is this healing? I'm not sure it is. I may know how to avert or control a catastrophic bleed but, if I haven't kept the woman and her partner informed of what is going on during the crisis, or helped them to understand what happened following the crisis, the couple may be left traumatised.

If by healing we mean 'to return somebody to health', have I actually achieved that? Is saving a life 'healing' in the true sense of the word or is it just patching somebody up so that they can continue to function? If I employ just the science, if I act as a body mechanic, my patient may go out into the world with the cracks loosely glued together so that she is in working condition – just. Given time, those loosely repaired cracks will become embedded with the grime of everyday living until they either develop into part of the beauty of who she is or until they mar the beauty of who she was. There is truth in the adage 'what doesn't kill you makes you stronger' but sometimes the killing is not instant and the strength is an optical illusion or a mask.

The effects of unaddressed trauma, whether physical or psychological, are thought to endure for years following the traumatising incident. If we reflect on the experience of the woman with the haemorrhage, she would probably have been filled with fear and horror, possibly feeling totally helpless and out of control during the event. Her partner, being in no position to help, would suffer those same emotions, perhaps to an even greater degree. To watch somebody in such crisis is deeply distressing, even if you are not close to them. How much worse then if it is all happening to somebody you love, and you are in no position to kiss it better?

Following the event, the couple may well have continued to endure those feelings of helplessness, each of them coping in the only way they know. Perhaps the man feels shame because he couldn't help his wife in her hour of greatest need and, just maybe, the woman feels angry with him for that very same reason. As they try to understand what has happened and comprehend why their once watertight relationship seems to be leaking, they may well be unable to sleep properly, which can lead in turn to excessive tiredness,

39

irritability and depression. The fact that the trauma happened during childbirth may mean that they can't cuddle one another to sleep as they used to because one or both of them is avoiding sexual intimacy. A hug in bed would be just too dangerous. If just one of them is avoiding lovemaking, the other will feel hurt and rejected; leading to anger, depression and low self-esteem.

And so it goes on. It becomes easy to see that, whilst a life may have been saved, well-being has not necessarily been achieved.

So, the medical model of healing doesn't really fulfil the criteria for this chapter although, without a doubt, it helps to keep us in working order. I think we can liken medics to washing-machine engineers; if the machine fails, a good engineer can diagnose which of the working parts is at fault and repair or replace it. The machine will work once again, albeit not to its full potential. That will depend on many variables – the temperature, the soap, the weight and composition of the load, how well the appliance is maintained … I'm sure you get the picture. The engineer can, of course, advise you of the factors needed for optimum performance but he won't be with you all the time to guide and remind you.

At the risk of alienating even further those medical colleagues with whom I work, I believe that we can equate medical schools with more highly developed versions of the old technical colleges. In their rudimentary training, the students learn the workings of the machine – how it is built, how it works and what can go wrong. As they become senior students they learn how to repair the machine, either by repairing or replacing old parts (surgery) or by modifying the machine's operating system (medicine). If there is a problem with the machine's fuzzy logic, the machine will be sent to an expert technician (psychiatry).

By expressing this view I don't mean to imply that medics perceive the person with whom they are dealing as a machine, far from it. I work and have worked with doctors who care deeply about their patients and who genuinely want to bring about the best outcome. The problem, as I see it, is that their training causes them to perceive the body as a machine of many parts, each part to be fixed by an expert in that particular branch of engineering. If the machine malfunctions, the doctor fixes it: orthodox medicine.

Alternative medicine

If orthodox medicine doesn't work then perhaps you opt for alternative medicine. There it is again, though, that word medicine – treatment of illness, not creation of a healthy whole. The alternative washing machine engineer may use a different set of tools but the outcome is the same – a functioning piece of equipment that may or may not work to its full potential. Ergo, healing and medicine are not interchangeable terms, medicine intimates intervention – a tinkering with the working parts of the machine rather than an absolute restoration of the whole.

More than medicine

So, in this book, I am not talking about medicine – alternative or otherwise. Rather, I want to explore with you the idea that there is something you can do for yourself that can make you feel better both physically and emotionally, and that will work alongside any other form of medicine that you may be receiving – something that is complementary to medicine but also something that is more than medicine. Conceivably, what we are discussing here could legitimately be thought of as a complementary therapy.

One of my editor's original observations was that, rather than controlling a thought process, I was engaging with it; running with it. I don't dispute that viewpoint but there is, I think, a valid reason for my taking this approach – I want to engage you in the thought processes that brought me to this point. I want you to understand that I thought deeply about my discovery regarding personal journaling as a route to well-being; I want you to understand what I thought and how I thought.

I need you to know too that I researched the reasons why writing is such a powerful tool for holistic health before I felt ready to share that information. Only by understanding for myself the reasons why my years of journaling have helped to keep me sane and well during a lifetime that would have caused many a strong person to despair, can I confidently pass on this knowledge to you. What you will read about in this chapter and those that follow is my personal belief system, one that has proved itself over forty plus years of writing and one that is now supported by growing research in the field.

I believe that our emotions are a direct result of the way we think. Why, for instance, can I be cast into a pit of despair when somebody comments on my weight gain when the same comment to a colleague would have no effect whatsoever? We think differently, that's why.

It has also been recognised for centuries that our emotions can have a direct effect on our physical well-being. If you suppress anger you may get a thumping headache, for instance. If we accept the above two points as correct, reasoning must lead us to deduce that our thought processes can make us ill. Or, conversely, they can help us to become well. I suppose, really, that encapsulates what I am trying to say – illness, or 'unwellness' can stem from the very thoughts you think; so if you can modify those thoughts, you can modify your health status. You can become well.

This book, then, is not about medicine. We need medicine. There is a place in this world for medicine. There is no place for medicine in this book.

The important corollary is that if you need medicine, you must go to a medic. The words I write cannot help you with the pure mechanics of your body but I do hope they will help you in achieving true physical and emotional wellness and the lightness of being that comes with functioning as an integrated whole.

Loss, Change and Grief

I don't know about you, but when I think of the word 'grief' the first thing that springs to mind is the death of somebody close and, of all our losses, this is probably the most significant one that we face. However, our lives are filled with loss. We may lose a job, a close friend might move far away, when we are young we lose boyfriends or girlfriends as a matter of routine. There is loss of status, loss of health, loss of memory, loss of a home, business or pet. Our reaction to all of these is grief. Each of these situations brings us to a watershed or changing point in our life. Sometimes the change required for us to assimilate the loss is relatively small but sometimes, as in the loss of a loved one, the changes we need to make may seem impossible.

Although there will be subtle differences in the way individuals feel grief, the process itself is universal. Despite this, when going through the process yourself you may fail to detect the all important signs and symptoms and, unfortunately, so might others. Keeping a journal is a valuable exercise because it demands that, at least whilst you are writing on its pages, you concentrate on yourself and your feelings, making it far more likely that you will identify where you are in the grief process and begin, perhaps unwittingly at first, to find your way through the maze of emotions that are assaulting you.

Grief is not something you 'get over'. Although when suffering loss we often focus on getting 'back to normal', we should appreciate that things can never be the same again, that this is the new normal. What eventually happens is that you learn to live within your new and different reality.

As we get older, of course, we are likely to experience loss more frequently. Not only do our children move away and start to live their own lives without us, but our friends and compatriots may also move away and, even more traumatically, some may die. And when someone that we know dies before they reach old age, we are forced to face the reality of our own mortality as well as dealing with the effects of loss and grief.

In this section of the book we will look at the various situations that may cause us to grieve and consider ways that writing might help us to cope.

9 *Bereavement*

How on earth do you assuage the bellowing pain of losing somebody you love? How do you fill that vast black void that has taken up residence in your chest and that threatens to envelope your whole being? I have to be completely honest here and say 'I really don't know'. What I can say with confidence, though, is that by expressing your sadness and rage on paper you are at least taking an active part in the grieving process rather than just letting it be something that happens to you.

There are a number of identified stages to the grief process, all of which need to be worked through in order to assimilate what has happened into the story of your life. The stages that resonate with me most are those described by Elisabeth Kübler-Ross in her 1969 book *On Death and Dying*. Recently this psychiatrist's work has come in for some criticism because there is no clear evidence to support the stages of grieving she cites. However, for me, there is truth in her hypothesis that when bereaved we will experience denial, isolation, anger, a desire to bargain with God, guilt and some form of depression before we finally come to accept what has happened. I recognise that we don't all go through the same stages in the same order but I'm willing to bet that we all experience these feelings at some time during our grieving process. In the Resources section (see page 174) I have included a table comparing five recent descriptions of the grieving process so that you can choose the one that resonates most with your own experience.

My own method of coming to some sort of an acceptance when my mother died was to take out the feelings one by one and write about them. I imagined that each feeling was a mysterious dark jewel that I held up to the window and

examined in minute detail. As I turned each jewel the
daylight would ignite tiny flashes of white light as it hit each
facet in turn. I held up many jewels to the light; some, like
the blood-red garnet of anger, were transparent and I could
see into them and through them. I was able to write about
that one with ease. Others, like the obsidian blackness of my
grief, took many months to flash back the white light of
understanding. Its opaque solidity seemed to resist my every
effort to get inside and understand it, almost as if it were
mocking me. Eventually, though, the bellowing pain reduced
to a shout and, after a while, became more of a whisper. It
remains at that level to this day. I still occasionally take out
the feelings to examine them but they don't scare me
anymore.

What I have described above may seem completely off the
wall to you. But such is the beauty of journaling, you can
imagine and write whatever you want, nobody need see it or
know about it except you. Initially, you may sit and look at
the blank page and not know how you are going to translate
the immensity of your feelings into words. Alternatively, you
may instantly let loose a stream of rage – at your loved one for
dying, at your god for allowing it to happen and at yourself
for allowing yourself to be this vulnerable. All are valid
reactions, all are normal and all will pass. If you continue
with the process you will find that, over time, as you sit with
pen in hand, your thoughts will begin to wander away from
the intensity of your grief. As you write, insights will come,
seemingly from nowhere, and you will begin to tap into your
deeper thoughts and emotions – and that is when the healing
will begin.

There are no rules to follow; write what you want to, when
you want to and how you want to. Forget the niceties of
punctuation and grammar (unless, like me, these matters are
of utmost importance to you). Be honest – sometimes the most
difficult person to be honest with is yourself; it is not always
agreeable to gaze at the real you, to confront the person
behind the mask. If you feel exposed and defenceless as you
write, you can be reassured that you are being honest. You
will cry. Sometimes the tears will be silent but sometimes you

may howl with grief – both are good. Muse over the good times and bad times spent with your loved one; what was it about that person that you loved and, conversely, what was it about that person that drove you to distraction? Write it all down, no holds barred. The exercises in this chapter will help to get you started.

Many people are moved to write poetry at times like this, even if they have never attempted to before. Up until my mother died, the only poem I had ever written was at infant school and was about dogs. Somehow, though, when my mum died, prose didn't seem to express the depth of my emotions. Eventually I wrote a number of poems, which achieved my objective of expressing the almost exquisite pain I was feeling. Because I suggest writing poetry in a number of the exercises in this book, I have included a short chapter on this subject that is intended to demystify the process (see page 33). You may think that you could never write poetry – don't be so sure. If it expresses how you are feeling inside, it has done its job.

The poem that follows was written during the angry stage of grieving for my mother. I'll never be a Poet Laureate but I think my anger shines through my words. More importantly, because I had to choose each word with care rather than just let the bile flow out of my pen, I found it helped me to shed light on my feelings rather than allow me to sink into a whirlpool of grief and negativity.

Angered, bereft and crying.

Darkness surrounds me and leaves me calling

endlessly for you,

like a frightened child,

grieving for a mother who will not hear.

How could you leave me,

knowing I still need you?

We spoke about the

joys we shared and the happy times we spent.

Then you kicked away my support and

left me lamenting for you,

my Mother.

Of course, grief doesn't only happen when a person dies. If that person has been ill and in pain for some time, death may even be a welcome release for all concerned. But how do you feel then? If you're anything like me, you feel a whole cocktail of emotions: a slug of grief at the loss served with a double guilt because you had wished the person dead, topped with a cherry of gratitude because the suffering has finally ended. You will drink the mixture in copious amounts until you are drunk with the pain. Then I suggest you write about it. I promise you that it helps.

Journaling through bereavement

Taking time to work through the grieving process will really help you. Acknowledging and dealing with your grief – without trying either to ignore it and pretend it does not exist, or indulge in it to the exclusion of all else – is the healthiest way through a difficult time.

This too will pass

Write about all the losses in your life – from childhood until now. As you write, try to recall the exact circumstances of the loss. Think about the following issues.

* ❀ Where you were.

* ❀ Who you were with.

* ❀ What you were wearing.

* ❀ How you were told.

* ❀ How old you were.

* ❀ Your immediate feelings.

* ❀ Your subsequent feelings.

* ❀ How that loss changed your life.

✤ Your feelings about that loss now.

As you write about these events, which were once so painful to you, you will find that, although the sadness remains, you have integrated the loss into your life and the pain is no longer sharp and unbearable.

Moments in time

When you are filled with longing and desperation for the presence of the person you have lost, capture the person's presence in writing. As you bring your loved one to mind, immerse yourself in the physical senses of being in the person's company. Remember a particular occasion you shared and write about it in the present tense.

✤ Where are you?

✤ What are you wearing?

✤ What is your loved one wearing?

✤ What can you see?

✤ What can you smell?

✤ What can you hear?

✤ What can you touch and what does it feel like?

✤ What are you feeling? Really search for the right word.

The piece of writing need not be very long, just a captured moment in time. You will find that it makes the person's presence almost palpable. When you have reached this depth of feeling, have a conversation with the person and write it in your journal. It will be imagined but, because you knew the person so well, it will feel authentic. If you do this exercise every time you are craving the company of your loved one you will find that you eventually build up a book of precious memories that faithfully illustrates the relationship you had with that person.

You can still talk to me

Shortly after my mother died I had a vivid dream. Most of the dream was unremarkable – I was just sitting on a bus talking to my mum about everyday stuff. The bit of the dream I remember clearly is the sudden realisation that I was talking to a dead person. I said to her, 'But you're dead!' She replied, 'Yes, I am dead, but that doesn't mean you can't still talk to me.' Because of the clarity of the dream I am convinced to this day that I really was having a conversation with my mother. That experience is the basis for this exercise.

* Imagine you are sitting with the person and having a normal everyday conversation.

* Write down what you would say.

* Write down the person's replies.

* In your journal, tell the person about your life now and how you have moved on since they died.

* Update the person on the lives of family and friends.

* Tell the person of your pain.

* In short, have a conversation in writing.

In undertaking this exercise you will find a way to tell the person all the stuff you want to share with them and, who knows, you may have a similar experience to the one I had in my dream. If the person's replies seem particularly bright in your mind, perhaps it's not all in your imagination.

Don't let the moments fade away

The beauty of a photograph is that it freezes a moment in time for ever; and sometimes, when you have lost somebody you love, you feel the need for proof that the person really existed. A photograph provides that proof. For this exercise you will need to find a picture of the person you have lost. When you have the photograph in front of you, write in your journal whilst thinking about the following:

* What is the person doing in the photograph?

50

❀ If you are in the photograph as well, what was the conversation immediately before and after the picture was taken?

❀ If there are other people in the photograph, who are they, are they still in your life today and what memories do you share with them?

❀ If you took the photograph, what were you saying to your loved one as you clicked the shutter?

❀ If it's a joyful photograph, what was it that you were so happy about or what were you laughing at?

❀ What was going on in your lives at the time the photograph was taken?

Moving forward

You need to be gentle with yourself and allow yourself some time to adjust to your changed world. This next exercise is very simple, but very important. Consider the following questions:

❀ How are you giving yourself time to recover?

❀ What do you need to help you cope?

❀ What could you do to help yourself feel better?

❀ What could you ask of others in the way of help?

As time goes by

As things begin to get easier for you – and I promise you that they will – you can begin the task of integrating the loss into your life. The following journal prompts may help you to do this:

❀ Write the story of your loved one's death and the feelings it evoked in you.

❀ Write the story of your loved one's life.

❀ Write about your life together.

✤ Write about the effect the person had on your own life. What did they teach you? Which of your qualities did they value? What about you caused them annoyance?

✤ Why do we die?

✤ What does it feel like to die?

✤ Where do we go when we die?

✤ What colour is death and why?

✤ What song lyrics remind you of your loved one?

Everybody hurts

The following are a collection of ideas for journaling that are relevant to anybody who has lost somebody they love.

✤ After the death of a loved one, everybody asks over and over again, 'Why?' 'Why did she die?' 'Why him, why me?' 'What did I do to deserve this pain?' Write your 'whys' in your journal. You may not be able to write the answers but it helps to write the question down as it somehow feels less pointless than just saying it over and over again in your mind.

✤ Is there a phrase that keeps coming to mind, such as, 'I will never see him grow up'. If there is, write it down, again as often as you wish.

✤ Express your anger. You will be angry with your loved one for dying, with your god for letting it happen, with the doctors for not saving her, with the world for being such an evil place. Write it all down. You will feel much better once you have.

✤ Express your pain and anger as a colour. Write about what it would look like as a painting. In fact, why not paint it? Try your hand at poetry using the suggestions from Chapter 7 (see page 33).

✤ What are your wishes for the future? Write a letter to the person you have lost about your hopes and fears, your aims and ambitions.

Use your experience

This is an exercise for helping somebody else who is troubled by the grief of having lost somebody dear.

✽ In your journal write down feelings that you remember experiencing when you lost somebody you loved. Try to relive the grief that you felt, remembering the almost physical pain at the centre of your being. Explore these feelings in as much depth as you can bear.

✽ Now that you can remember the soul-agony of this experience, write to your friend. Do not put all of your pain into words, after all, this is her time to grieve and you should not rob her of this special time by referring to your own past experiences. But, having done the journaling exercise, you will be in a position to empathise, so that when you say something like 'I promise that the black hole in your heart will eventually close', you can say it and know it to be true.

10 The Death of a Child

Children aren't supposed to die. In the natural course of events they are supposed to live longer than their parents. You are supposed to watch them grow and develop. You expect your parents to die before you but you never really believe that you will experience the death of your child, other than in your worst nightmares. To lose a child is to lose your future, to lose opportunities that can never be grasped and memories that can never be made.

I am grateful to say that I have never experienced this particular grief and, to those of you who have, I ask that you forgive me for daring to write about a pain and anguish that is beyond description and imagination. I envisage a rage so profound that it threatens to destroy you, a pain so deep that there is nothing left inside. Then, after what is deemed to be a suitable period of time, you are advised to move on with your life, to smile and laugh again. Perhaps the people who advise you to do so do not realise that, for the rest of your life, you will continue to be the parent of the child who has gone. Maybe it is only you who knows that you will continue to love your son or daughter with all your being, and yet are dispossessed of the right to show that love openly.

My instincts are that the grieving for a lost child is a lifelong journey, a scary and lonely passage that never really ends. Indeed, it may feel that letting go of the grief is being disloyal to the child – while the grief continues, the child survives. Perhaps that is why we poke at the wound following a death, never letting a scab form, forever keeping the damage raw and bleeding, and the pain fresh in our soul.

If you have never kept a journal before, perhaps now is the time to start. Write down your memories, write about the hopes you had for your child and about the fears you have now. Write about the emptiness you feel inside and berate your god for allowing this obscenity. Stick special photographs in your journal along with other souvenirs if you have any – a flower you've kept, a mother's day card, a cot tag. All of these things are concrete evidence that your child lived and loved. Eventually, you will find that you are writing about your hopes and plans for the future. And one day, in that future that you cannot yet imagine, you will look back at your journal and realise how far you have come.

You may find that some of the exercises in the previous chapter are useful, but the ones that follow are aimed specifically at those who want to write through the pain of losing a child. They have been designed to help you whether you have had a miscarriage early in pregnancy, given birth to a stillborn child or lost a child who has been with you for some time.

Journaling when a child dies

Hopes and dreams

Most women, when they discover they are pregnant, start dreaming and planning for the life that is growing inside of them and, when your child dies, these hopes and dreams die too. Use the following prompts to write about these dreams in your journal.

- ❊ When and how did you find out you were pregnant?

- ❊ Who was the first person you told? What words did you use and what was the reaction?

- ❊ How did you feel about being pregnant? What thoughts went through your mind?

- ❊ What did it feel like being pregnant? Did you suffer from morning sickness or any strange food cravings?

- ❊ Did you fall in love with the child inside you straightaway or did it take you a while to get used to the fact that there were two of you?

* Did you take special measures to ensure that you and the baby inside you remained healthy?

* How did your partner feel about becoming a father and, if you have other children, how did they feel?

The moment your dreams came crashing down

If you lost your child in pregnancy, it must have felt that your whole world had changed within a moment of time. Maybe you got up that morning pregnant and went to bed with your hopes and dreams destroyed. Use the following prompts:

* Where were you when you learned about your baby's death? Who was with you, who told you and how did you react?

* Write a letter to your baby – including the information that you wrote for the last exercise. Also tell the baby of your grief, how mummy and daddy cried and how upset grandma and granddad were.

* What choices did you need to make? Why and how did you make them? Tell your baby about it.

* What happened to your body after your baby died and were you surprised by the physical changes?

The body mends but the mind takes longer

It takes your body about six weeks to return to normal after a pregnancy has ended, but it can take your mind a lot longer. After six weeks or so have passed, write about the following topics in your journal:

* What can you remember about your feelings at the time of the loss?

* What are your feelings now?

* What is your most intense feeling?

* What about the people around you – how do they react to you now?

* Who do you feel has helped you most during this time?

❀ What is it that that person has done that has particularly helped you?

As the first anniversary of your baby's death rolls round, consider the following writing prompts:

❀ On the date that your baby was due, write a letter to him telling him what has happened in your life since he died and how you feel about him.

❀ Mark the anniversary by writing down your feelings on leaves or petals, one word on each, and scatter them in a place that holds some meaning for you.

❀ There will be times over the years when you will find yourself thinking about your baby, how old he would be now, what he would be doing now, what he would look like. When these feelings take hold, write them in your journal.

You will always be the mother of your baby, even though he died. By keeping a journal based on these exercises, you will be honouring the fact that he existed, that you loved him and that he still has a place, no matter how secret, in your heart.

Silent birth

At each stillbirth I have had the privilege to attend, the one aspect that has affected me more than any other is the silence. In a normal delivery room, birth is a noisy event. I am surrounded by the cries of the baby, the expressions of wonder from the birth partner and the exhausted tears of delight from the mother. Conversely, when a birth is also a death, there is no lusty cry from the baby and no wonder and delight from the birth partner. If there are sounds at all, they are the quiet sobs of the mother and the sad, hushing sounds of the midwife.

Of course, all of the above journaling ideas are relevant for you but here are some more prompts that you may find useful:

❀ Did you know your baby had died before you went into labour?

❀ What was your labour like? Who was there to support you? What thoughts went through your mind?

❀ Describe the room in which your child was born. What could you see, smell, touch and hear?

❀ Describe the midwife. What did she look like? Describe her voice. Was she softly spoken? Did she have an accent? What did she do that you found particularly helpful or particularly hurtful? What did she say to you? Did she cry with you? What was her name and what did she tell you about herself?

❀ Did you see your baby as soon as she was born, or did you wait a while because you were worried about what she would look like?

❀ How much did she weigh? What did she look like? Describe her face, her body, her hair. Stillborn babies usually have the most beautiful rosebud mouths. Did yours?

❀ What did you say to your child, either in your mind or out loud?

❀ Did you have a special memorial service for your baby? Who was present? What did they say?

❀ Did you hold your baby or bath her? Describe how that felt.

❀ How long after the birth did you leave the hospital and what were your first thoughts on returning home?

❀ Who came to see you and who wrote to you expressing their sadness? What did you find particularly helpful?

When writing these things, really go inside yourself and pull out the memories. Concentrate on sights, sounds, smells and the way things felt under your fingers. It might be painful to do these things but exploring what happened in such depth will help you to put the events into some sort of order in your mind. Only when you have done that will you begin to heal.

11 *Losing a Child when a Relationship Ends*

Any parent who has lost a child as the result of the breakdown of a relationship knows the extreme trauma and pain that this experience brings. Anything that can help you sort this out in your mind has to be of value. Your soul feels the whole gamut of emotions: guilt, grief, pain, anger and depression, and your mind lingers on the what-ifs.

In my own case, I made a considered decision that my child would have a better quality of life if she lived with her father and his new wife. My own life was chaotic in the extreme and certainly not a fit environment for a three-year-old child. I did this in the 1970s, when views weren't quite as liberal as they are now, and not only did I suffer the anguish of what I'd done but I also had to endure barbed comments and, sometimes, out and out nastiness from people who should have known better.

Did it get any easier? No, not really. Obviously, I don't wander round in sackcloth and ashes, bemoaning my fate, and a busy life means that the situation is not constantly at the forefront of my thoughts. But birthdays, Christmas and family occasions still leave me with an achy heart.

Of course, to a certain extent, my pain was self-inflicted. If I'd been a stronger person perhaps I would have sorted my life out and ensured that it was a suitable environment for my young daughter. A 'what-if' par excellence! What must you feel then, if the decision wasn't made by you but by the courts? I can't begin to imagine, but would hazard a guess that added to the pain I experienced would be a generous helping of anger combined with a feeling that your life is totally out of your control.

Unfortunately, children are often the silent victims of divorce and are sometimes even used as bargaining tools. This sad fact isn't helped by the legal process that begins with the end of a marriage, and in which the children tend to be seen as assets of the marriage, along with the house, the dishwasher and the CD collection.

In such a combative system as the divorce courts, it's no wonder that people end up hurt and angry and, no matter how hard you try to conceal your true feelings towards your ex-spouse, your child will instinctively know the truth of how you feel. For this reason, I have included some exercises to help you try to resolve whatever angry feelings you have towards your ex-partner as well as those to help you deal with being the absent parent.

I hope that the following suggestions will help you to clarify your thoughts and bring you some peace of mind.

Journaling through the loss of a child when a relationship ends

It is essential that you deal with your inevitable anguish so that you can move on in your life. At first this may seem impossible, but be assured that things will change for the better.

Write your pain and anger

A simple and possibly painful exercise is to write about your feelings in your journal. Start with one of the suggested words in the list below and just write down whatever pops into your head, whether it is single words or complete phrases, sentences or paragraphs. This technique is known as free writing. Do not censor your thoughts; write whatever comes to mind. Because this is likely to be hard work emotionally, I suggest you limit your writing time to 20 minutes at the most.

* Anger.

* Guilt.

* Pain.

❋ What will I miss about not having my child constantly in my life?

❋ What will my child miss about not having me there all the time?

For the last two prompts it is likely that you will become angry, but this is the whole point. Expressed anger is healthy, and internalised anger is dangerous. If you find that your overriding feelings are of anger, then you should try some of the exercises in Chapter 21 (see page 124) that deal exclusively with this emotion.

Write to your child

You are not going to send this letter and it is important to bear that in mind. The time to write a letter that you will send to your child is when you have dealt with your own emotions. The letter you write for this exercise could, however, form the basis of a more coherent and well-thought out letter when the time is right.

In your letter you may express the depth of your feelings and the pain that you feel, and you can tell your child exactly what it is you will miss about her. Document your memories: good, bad and funny. Tell her exactly what your feelings were when she was born and describe what she looked like and how she felt in your arms. What you are doing is validating your parenting of your child, and committing to paper and to memory the love that you felt then and that you will continue to feel.

Your story

If you are creative, start a 'Your Story' book. Write the story of your child's life from the day she was born. If you have photographs, stick them in. Decorate the pages with illustrations; it doesn't matter if you can only draw matchstick men. Find quotes and poems that express how you feel. If you can write your own poems, do so. When you think of your child, instead of just mulling things over, write a letter to her in the journal, expressing your thoughts in terms that she would be able to understand.

You have a choice as to what to do with this book. You can either use it in the knowledge that your child will never see it, in which case your writing can be as unexpurgated as you wish, or you can put it together with the aim of giving it to the child when she is, say, 18 years old.

We both still love you

This truth that is often said to children at the end of a relationship is not always easy for a child to understand, particularly when the parents are still at war. A child will find it much easier to accept it as truth if you and your partner manage to bury the hatchet. In order to be able to do this effectively, you will need to explore your feelings surrounding your ex-partner and try to remember the reasons why you were involved with each other in the first place. I am not going to pretend that this is an easy task. Obviously, for some couples it will be easier than it is for others. If your partner has betrayed you in some way, then you are going to have to work very hard on this one. Start with these prompts:

* Write three good things about your ex.

* Write three good things about yourself.

* Write about the areas of parenting that your partner is better at than yourself.

* Write about the areas of parenting that you are better at than your partner.

When your child needs something doing that your ex is better at than you are, you will know, because you have already planned it in your journal, that this is an opportunity to praise the other parent by saying something along the lines of, 'Oh, Daddy is really good at that, far better than me, why don't you ask him?' It will go much further towards having a happy child than either playing the martyr and trying to do everything yourself or bad mouthing the absent parent for not being around when you need him.

The other thing you will need to do is agree with your ex a set of ground rules to protect the children as much as possible from your emotional fallout. In your journal, spend some time writing down what you think the ground rules should be. By journaling these first before discussing them with your ex, you will have had a chance to work through the emotions involved. If your ex disputes them with you, you will also have the confidence of having thought them through thoroughly beforehand. You might consider the following important points.

* ❋ Never criticise the other parent in front of the child.

* ❋ Never ask your child to keep secrets from the other parent.

* ❋ Never ask your child to choose between the two of you.

12 Marriage, Relationships and Divorce

When we marry or enter a long-term relationship I don't think any of us seriously consider that it might end in separation or divorce. We enter the relationship with hopes, dreams and plans for the future, and these are exactly what we lose when it all comes to an end. Generally, the deterioration in a long-term committed relationship is a slow process and, despite areas of the partnership being less than perfect, most of us carry on, feeling that we have made too big a commitment to give up easily and without a fight. Gradually, as the relationship worsens, it can seem as if bits of you are actually dying and you can find yourself tolerating much more than you would have done before you entered the relationship.

There are usually signs that the partnership is dysfunctional before one or other of the partners considers bringing it all to an end, and the first of these is termed in clinical jargon 'unpleasant interactions'. This innocent little phrase can cover anything from simply arguing to constant criticism or continually being corrected by your partner, both of which are sure fire ways to erode your self-esteem. Other issues that crop up include lack of intimacy (and by that I mean emotional intimacy rather than sexual closeness) and poor conflict resolution. You will find exercises for dealing with all of these issues at the end of this section.

Facing the end of a relationship, you are torn between doing what you think you should do, that is, stay and be less than happy, or doing what you would really like to do, which is escape and reclaim your life. Going through this dilemma recently, I kept hearing my father's voice in my head counselling me to draw up a list of advantages and disadvantages. Every time I heard his voice, I gave a wry, inward smile and pushed the thought aside as being ludicrous. Thinking on it though, it wasn't such a bad idea. Advantages and disadvantages may be a bit too simplistic but writing things down, as always, will certainly help to clarify the thought process. In the Resources section you will find the template for a cost/benefit analysis (see page 175), which is simply an upmarket way of writing out advantages and disadvantages.

In my own situation, I didn't really know what was wrong with my relationship and so I blamed it on my partner's past behaviour. Whilst that behaviour had indeed been reprehensible, it was in the past. The breakthrough that I came to after months of journaling was that nobody can make me unhappy but myself. My partner can do things that I don't like or that hurt me but it is me who chooses to feel unhappy and hurt.

If you're reading this section because you think your relationship is at an end, I suggest that you try the following exercises before you make any irretrievable decisions or changes to your life.

Journaling when your relationship is in trouble

We make use of the Rational Emotive Behaviour and Cognitive Behaviour models for these exercises, and perhaps in a long-term relationship is where they're most useful.

How many of us have a tendency to blame our partners for making us feel bad? It is vital to remember that each relationship consists of two individuals. The trick of Cognitive Behaviour models is to help us to understand that nobody can make us feel bad but ourselves.

Identify your demands

The journaling described below is designed to help you discover what it is you are expecting of yourself, your partner and your relationship. Your writings on this topic could give you the first clue or reinforce your growing belief that you are in a dysfunctional relationship. It will require a good deal of deep thinking but could nip potential serious relationship problems in the bud.

❈ Make a list of everything you believe you *must* bring to the relationship or do within it, for instance:

* Must you gain your partner's approval for everything you do?

* Must you alone be responsible for keeping the house nice?

* Is it down to you alone to make the relationship succeed?

❈ Make a list of everything you believe your partner *must* bring to the relationship, for instance:

* Must your partner approve of everything you do for the relationship to survive?

* Must your partner provide you with undivided attention at all times?

* Must your partner like to do the same things as you?

❈ Make a list of everything you think your relationship *must* bring to your life, for instance:

* If the relationship is going through a sticky phase must that mean that life is no good?

* Must the relationship provide for all the spiritual needs for both you and your partner?

* Must the relationship be the only source of friendship for both of you?

The above *musts* are only a selection of some of the beliefs that many of us have about our relationships and, if you consider them in any depth, you will realise that they are unrealistic.

When you have your lists, write about why you believe these things; is it because of the outcome of past relationships or is it, perhaps, something to do with your childhood? Once you have discovered where these beliefs have come from you can start disputing them, again in your journal. Ask yourself what evidence there is to support your *musts* and, when you can find none, try to reframe your thinking about the issue.

As explained in the chapter on talking therapies (see page 16), we can make this process as simple as ABC. You may find it helpful to use the template provided (see page 168).

Of course, it all looks very simple when written down as ABC and, once you've got the hang of it, it *is* simple. Prepare yourself for a bit of uneasiness though as you write about your unrealistic and possibly irrational beliefs and begin to gain an understanding of the part *you* have played in the gradual erosion of your relationship.

Soothing days and mutual support

This is a very easy and pleasurable exercise. Make a list of simple things that you would like your partner to do for you and ask him to do the same. Each day you should both try to do one of the things on the list, which will result in both of you feeling more supported within your relationship.

It's not all bad

As the dysfunction within your relationship progresses unnoticed, or noticed but not addressed, you may find that you lose sight of positive aspects of your partner's personality. In your journal write about his positive traits. Do this over a number of days and make each trait the subject of a ten-minute timed writing. Nobody is all bad; try to remember what it was you initially fell in love with.

Keep a couple's journal

You might have to do the hard sell on this one, but it's worth it.

Within a journal you can find the space to explore one another's thoughts, feelings and perceptions. Somehow, it can be easier to write things down than to say them directly to the other person, especially if the things you want to say may cause the other to feel some pain or sadness. The other beauty of journaling as a couple is that it allows the individuals within the relationship space to be exactly that, an individual. So often, in relationships the boundaries between where one half of the couple ends and the other half begins can become blurred. Whilst this is what marriage is all about, it can also impede personal growth and individuality, which in turn can deaden a relationship.

Whilst it is not essential that you both contribute the same amount to the journaling, it is essential that you are both committed to the endeavour. If you set goals and objectives within the journal, these must be agreed by both partners, and both partners need to make the same commitment to achieving these aims. It is up to you when you choose to write in your journal but it works best when you set aside a specific time for journaling on a regular basis.

You will find that writing down your feelings and perceptions stimulates further discussion (and sometimes debate) on a far deeper level than previously. If both of you are wholly committed to this process, both participate and both take it seriously, the intimacy levels within your relationship will soar.

One step at a time

This exercise is designed to help save a relationship where you are already aware of the cracks. Write down three things you want to change about your relationship but try to focus on the positive rather than the negative. So, instead of writing 'I want him to stop doing x', think more along the lines of what you would like him to start doing.

Set goals for these changes. Read the chapter on personal

growth (see page 145) and use some of the goal-setting techniques described there.

Journaling through the end of a relationship

You've done all you can to try to save your marriage – you've even done the above exercises and you're still convinced that the relationship is staggering to its inevitable conclusion. You are facing what will probably be one of the most stressful events of your life. By learning to understand the emotional stresses that you are under, you will be in a better position to deal with them. You also need to remember that every ending contains within it a new beginning; not only will you survive this period in your life but you might well find you thrive because of it.

If you have instigated the split, you may be filled with feelings of guilt; if you did not instigate it you will probably feel hurt and bitter. Whichever of these is your position, you will undoubtedly feel frightened, hurt, lonely and resentful. You may also miss the companionship, financial security and, if there was still a sexual relationship at the end, you will miss the reassurance that gave you of your continued attractiveness and desirability. If the children are with you, you may feel bitter because your freedom will be curtailed but, if they are with your partner, you will feel guilty and worry that they will stop loving you.

What a mess! But you can get through it, probably coming out the other side stronger, more confident and infinitely wiser. I hope that the exercises that follow will not only help you to cope, but that they will make sure you thrive rather than just survive.

Honour your feelings

Our instinct, when in pain, is to try to bury the painful feelings. Don't do it! You are feeling the pain for a reason and the reason is that you need to integrate this experience into your life. I am not saying that you should wallow in your despair, although I have gone down that route in the past and I think it probably helps you to get the grief over and done with more quickly.

This exercise involves you thinking about the details of the relationship and the break-up. Write in your journal your answers to the following questions:

* ❁ What will you miss about your partner and your time together?

* ❁ What will you be pleased has ended? For instance, did you hate it when he went on and on about a pet project or hobby?

* ❁ You will be feeling angry. What is it you are angry about?

* ❁ You will, of course, be very sad. What saddens you most?

* ❁ What are your fears surrounding the break-up? For instance, are you scared of living alone?

Write a letter

Whether we've been rejected or whether we've been the one to end a relationship, it's difficult to say what's in our heart. The spoken word just doesn't seem to do justice to the strength of feeling that you are experiencing. Write a letter to your partner explaining your grief in depth. You are never going to send this letter, so be as melodramatic as you like. Just let it all pour out of you. This exercise will help you to explore feelings that you might have difficulty admitting to.

Move forward

I don't know when it will happen for you but there will come a day when, actually, you feel a bit bored with all this misery. You will feel fed up with not taking care of your appearance and with staying in and watching the telly. If you're a mum, you will begin to feel that you want time to yourself away from the home. Basically, you will begin to feel human again.

However, whilst the desire to move forward will be strong, there will be a certain amount of fear and trepidation attached to this. For this exercise, explore in your journal exactly what it is that is stopping you from moving on; this could be just one fear or a number of fears. You may feel inadequate, unattractive, scared of being hurt again, or you may just not know where to start. Write about these fears and think about ways to overcome the obstacles you are putting in your way.

The following is an example of how you might journal this, although in reality I imagine that your journal entries would be more detailed and far longer.

* Nobody else is going to want me. I'm fat, ugly and undesirable.

* Why do I feel like this? Because my ex made disparaging remarks about my looks.

* Dispute it. Think about why he loved you in the first place, and perhaps give a thought to whether you can improve your image for your own benefit.

Value yourself

If my answers to the previous exercise are in anyway similar to yours, it would be a good idea to start rebuilding your self-esteem. Do some timed writings of about ten to 20 minutes on the following topics:

* What have you done today/this week/this year to make you feel proud?

* What is about you that your mum is proud of?

* If your closest friend were asked to write a character reference about you, what would she say?

* Make a list of the people who love you.

This exercise should make you realise just how wonderful you are. Celebrate it.

Don't view your relationship through rose-tinted glasses

When you are in the process of breaking up it seems that all you do is focus on the negative. When the relationship is ended, the reverse is true. Time and loneliness filter out the bad times, a bit like when somebody dies and you forget all the person's bad traits. Again, do some timed writing in your journal on the following:

* List five things (or more) that you found really annoying about your partner.

* List all the things you felt were missing from the relationship.

* If you could have made your ex into your perfect partner, what would have needed changing?

Recognising the lessons

When you're ready, and only you will know when the time is right, write in your journal about what you have learned from this stage of your life. Here are some prompts:

* What have I learned about myself?

* What have I learned about relationships?

* What have I learned about life?

* What have I learned about the opposite sex?

* What did I give to the relationship?

* How did I contribute to the end of the relationship?

* What would I do differently next time?

* What new interests and skills did I gain from our time together?

Although at the beginning it feels as if your heartbreak will last forever, if you work your way through all of the above exercises, when you are ready to move on, you will do so with greater confidence and greater knowledge of yourself and life.

13 Losing Your Job

When I was growing up in 1950s and 1960s England, there was such a thing as a job for life. Youngsters leaving school were encouraged to go into the public sector, becoming nurses or teachers or joining the civil service; these were the sort of jobs that were considered to last a lifetime. Nowadays it is highly unlikely that when you retire it will be from the job you took on leaving full-time education.

It is very common these days to have one or even two career changes during a working lifetime. Whilst to some that seems like a loss of security, to others it is a promise of a more fulfilling life. I have to say I subscribe to the second point of view because I am a very different person at 50 to the young woman I was at 18 – or at least I hope I am.

For many, a change of direction in their working life may be thrust upon them by events outside of their control – the company they work for may be downsized, or merge with another company. The skills they possess may be overtaken by technology or factored out to another company. In the United Kingdom, at the end of 2005, there were a total of 1.41 million people out of work – many of them in the manufacturing industries.

The problem for those losing their job is that working doesn't just bring home the bacon; it also provides a sense of purpose, self-esteem and status in life. The other things to go when a job is lost are daily routines and relationships, which can leave you feeling completely surplus to requirements. The loss of a job is such a powerful event that individuals can find themselves undergoing exactly the same grief process as described in the chapter on bereavement. What's more, the loss of a job doesn't just affect the person who has experienced the loss, but it also impacts on their family and partner. That is why some people go out each day at the same time for months after the loss has occurred, too scared and ashamed to tell their partner what has happened. They cling on in the vain hope that they may find alternative employment and never have to admit to the truth.

Possibly the worst thing you can do in this situation is to bottle things up and try to deal with your feelings and fears alone. It is likely that the depth of your feelings will make it difficult for you to make sensible decisions or to take action, and this is where journaling can be a useful tool to enable you to move forward. Losing your job can leave you feeling as if you've failed and it is likely that you will turn your perceived failures over and over in your mind, so the first step is to get you feeling a little more positive. The first exercise below is designed to help you achieve this. Once you are feeling more positive, you need to think strategically about how to move on from this stage in your life. As ever, writing can help you to do this and the following exercises will enable you to use your journal effectively at this difficult time.

Journaling when you have lost your job

It is important to remember that you are not your job; your job is only a part of who you are. It is also vital to think about how you move on from this low point, perhaps not today and perhaps not tomorrow, but soon. The following exercises are designed to help with these two issues.

I have been successful

You may not have made a million but there will have been some successes in your job. Use the following questions to write about these successes:

* ❉ What will your workmates miss about you?

* ❉ Think of a person at work who likes you and then write down what it is they like about you.

* ❉ What positive results did you have at work, based on your own efforts?

❀ What assets did you bring to your job?

Now widen the exercise to write about successes in your life outside of your job. The purpose of this exercise is not only to make you feel good about yourself; it might also help you to identify additional skills that could assist you in your search for work.

Miracles result from hard work

You may feel that you need something incredible to happen for you to get out of this current situation. The fact is, however, that nothing will get you out of this current situation – you have to get yourself out of it. Start visualising what it is you want from the future and then work towards it. Clarify your vision by writing it in your journal, using the following prompts:

❀ Do I actually enjoy what it is I do for a living?

❀ Is there anything else I would rather do?

❀ Do I have the necessary skills to do this? If not, how can I attain these skills?

❀ What can I do *right now* to begin the move forward?

❀ What other steps do I need to take?

❀ Can I do this alone or do I need help?

❀ Where can I find that help?

Remember, the above are only prompts to start you thinking; to get maximum benefit you need to write in depth and detail about these issues.

What do I want from my next job?

Be proactive here; think about exactly what it is you want your job to bring to your life. Explore the following prompts in your journal:

❀ How much do I need to earn before I consider myself financially successful?

❀ What does status mean to me?

❀ Is the social interaction that comes from a job important to me or would I rather work alone?

❀ Do I think having authority is important?

❀ Where do I believe self-fulfilment comes from?

Feelings

Write a few sentences about what the following trigger words mean to you in the context of your job loss:

❀ Fear.

❀ Anger.

❀ Failure.

❀ Relief.

❀ Happiness.

❀ Sorrow.

❀ Loneliness.

❀ Vengefulness.

❀ Excitement.

❀ Powerlessness.

❀ Shock.

Sell yourself

Take a good look at your curriculum vitae and decide if you really are showing yourself off to your best advantage. Lists of schools, colleges and previous employers are all well and good but they don't show any prospective employers who you are and what benefits you can bring to their company. Brainstorm these things in your journal:

❀ Are you a good team player? Are you a natural leader?

❀ Do you have any outside interests that would make a positive contribution to working life?

Now use what you have written to update your CV.

14 Losing a Friend

I met Carol on the interview day for midwifery training. There had been over 600 applicants for 20 places and this was the final hurdle. Emotions were high, we were all strangers and we were all very wary – everybody in that room was a potential competitor and a potential colleague. The interviews were arranged to be part of a day-long process during which there were talks and videos describing what it was like to be a midwife. Coffee and meal breaks were taken in the hospital canteen and involved that embarrassing procedure of deciding whom to sit with when part of a group of strangers.

One girl sat alone, the others were in larger groups from which false and embarrassed laughter rang out. The loner was tall and elegant looking, in a blue suit decorated with a simple gold brooch. Her hair was immaculately styled into a neat blonde bob and her make-up was understated and well applied. By comparison, I must have looked like the local village idiot – short and dumpy with masses of unruly golden hair. And although I know that I would have tried hard to look smart and presentable, I have never been blessed with very good dress sense.

So, what a choice: I could make embarrassed, polite conversation with a group of females I had never met and who were cackling like witches around a cauldron; I could sit in the shade of Mrs Elegant's style and sophistication or I could make myself feel like Billie No-Mates by sitting alone. I chose to sit with Mrs Elegant. The first thing I noticed was that her mascara was smudged beneath the left eye, which delighted me and allowed me to smile smugly to myself – obviously she wasn't so perfect after all.

It was six years before we stopped talking – although clearly we took time off for study, work and partners. We felt we were soul mates of the platonic kind; I admired and respected her and, allegedly, she felt the same about me. If there was anybody in the world I wanted to emulate it was Carol and, once again, she felt the same about me. We had both left our child when leaving their fathers, we both loved to flirt with the opposite sex and we could both drink gin for England. A match made in heaven; it was pity that neither of us had lesbian tendencies. She was the closest and most trusted female friend I have ever had and I miss her to this day.

So what happened? She moved to Cornwall. We cried and promised to keep in touch and never let the friendship die and, for a while, we did just that. But inevitably she made new friends and I learned to live my life without her. Two years after Carol moved, I also moved with my family to the West Country. I live about two hours' drive from Carol and her husband, but only twice in six years have we seen one another. On the occasions when we did meet up the relationship continued as if there had been no break but, when we parted and went back to our own lives, there was no black hole where the other used to be. We now send occasional e-mails but too much time has passed and too much water has flowed under the bridge, I think, for us to regain the intensity of friendship we once had. It saddens me and, because I know her so well, I know it saddens her too.

So what is it about friendship that is so special? There is no doubt that Carol and I loved one another, but it was a different sort of love to that which we felt for our partners or our parents. Our relationship was intimate in that she knew stuff about me that nobody else knows; she knew of my past misdemeanours, my sexual exploits, my hang-ups, my frustration with my marriage; she could see beyond my bluff and bluster to the frightened little girl inside. I could count on her to be honest and, if she disapproved of something I had done or was planning to do, she would let me know in her blunt Lancashire manner. And that, I think, is the crux of friendship. It allows a sharing of views and ideas without threatening the fabric of the relationship. If my husband disapproves of something I do, it can have lasting repercussions on our relationship – especially if, despite his disapproval, I continue to do whatever it is anyway. If a friend disapproves, we'll discuss it but if I continue with my action, the friendship is not in any danger – we'll just agree to differ.

When my friendship with Carol faded I lost my partner in crime, my counsellor, my fashion advisor, my personal comedienne and my fan-club. No wonder it was such a painful process, a process that does not yet appear to be over, even though what I have described happened many years ago.

Some of the articles I've read during my research have likened a deep female friendship to marriage. Back in the eighteenth century, friendship was a male domain and we see the remnants of this in the all-male drinking clubs that are still to be found in our big cities. However, since time began there has always been a special bond between women and, in biblical times and in some present-day ethnic communities, special rooms are set aside for women for use during childbirth and menstruation.

Of course, not all friendships are beneficial and not all friendships end. The writing prompts below are designed to give you some insight into your friendships and to discover the role they play in your life. Additionally, it is just as valid for you to do some bereavement exercises at the end of a friendship as it is for any other loss in your life. Rather than exercises *per se*, what follows are some ideas and thoughts surrounding friendship for you to think and write about. As you do this, other aspects of friendship will probably occur to you, some of which may help you to decide to 'end it or mend it'.

Journaling your friendships

Friendship is important to everyone and you can use your journal to find out more about how important particular friendships are to you and how to improve on those that are not working so well.

Your friendship style

This exercise will enable you to explore your own personal style of friendship – what sort of friend you are and what you expect from a friendship. You may find this helpful if you are experiencing difficulties in this area.

* ❋ What do I look for in a friendship?

* ❋ What am I prepared to give to a friendship?

* ❋ My friend has told me she is moving away. How do I feel?

* ❋ My friend has unwittingly upset me with something she said. How do I feel and how would I deal with this?

* ❋ My friend is having troubles in her marriage and has come to me for advice. How would I act and what would I say?

* ❋ My friend has appalling clothes sense but doesn't seem to realise this. Do I tell her and, if I do, how would I do this?

* ❋ My friend has told me that she is considering having an affair. How does that make me feel and what would I say to her?

* ❋ When I am with my friend I feel ...

* ❋ My friend makes me feel good about myself by ...

* ❋ My friend makes me feel bad about myself by ...

* ❋ When my partner talks to me about my friend he says ...

* ❋ When my partner says negative things about my friend I feel ...

Friendship for the disheartened

You would think that friendship comes naturally, wouldn't you? A straw poll amongst my colleagues and associates though would suggest that this is a flawed notion. Using the following prompts, write for ten to 20 minutes:

❀ Why would anybody want to be my friend?

❀ I don't have time for friends because ...

❀ If I make friends I risk ...

❀ If I don't make friends I risk ...

❀ When a friend disagrees with one of my ideas, I feel ...

At the end of the writing you will be amazed at just how threatening friendships can sometimes be. What I want you to realise is that, if you feel like this, you can be sure that many hundreds of other people feel the same way. These feelings can cause an obstacle to the development of close, secure friendships.

Your next writing task is to dispute all of the negatives you wrote in the above exercise.

15 Losing Your Health

Most of us, I think, take good health for granted. We don't think about an organ or place in our body until it either starts to hurt or ceases to work. Even transient and minor ailments like a summer cold can cause us to realise how we undervalue the miracle of a body in full working order. Imagine then how it feels to be told that the pain you are suffering, the difficulty you have breathing, or the sadness you are feeling, is not transient but permanent. My own experience is that as well as the grief over the loss of once perfect health, this situation brings feelings of stress over possible loss of employment together with guilt and negativity because, 'maybe the illness isn't as bad as I'm making out and people will think I'm just being lazy'.

This chapter is not about health itself but about dealing with the loss of health and the impact that has on our self-perception. Journaling about illness is discussed in the section on physical health (see page 129).

There have been two pivotal moments in my life when I have had to face the loss of health, once for my son and once for myself. On both occasions the health problems had been long-standing before identification and, although the symptoms had been inconvenient and troublesome, they had been a fact of life and, therefore, incorporated into our everyday family existence. Along with formal diagnosis, however, came grief, anger and pain. For me then, it wasn't the illness itself that was difficult to come to terms with but what the illness did to my self-perception and my perception of my child.

Personal experience

When my youngest son was born I fell instantly in love. It had been a difficult and painful delivery due to his size and his position in my uterus. It became clear on his second day of life that I was not the only one to have suffered during his birth; where his head had been wedged against my spine during the process he had developed what looked like half a policeman's helmet on his head. I was reassured by the midwives that this was a just a *cephalhaematoma* that would soon go down and that there was nothing to worry about. It seemed they were right because by his first week's anniversary there was no sign of any deformity; he was, it seemed, a perfectly healthy and normal child. The policeman's helmet was something remembered only by me, and faded into family folklore.

As my older son had suffered from hyperactivity, life with Will seemed relatively peaceful. He wasn't climbing up the curtains or kicking the long-suffering dog each time he passed by; on the contrary, he played with his huge box of model cars for most of the day. The game was always the same: he would drive the cars into the car park and park them neatly in size order, where he would leave them whilst he watched his current favourite video over and over again. A particular video would be his favourite for a period of weeks and he would watch nothing else. Eventually, he would choose another from the well-stocked shelves as his favourite and the original 'favourite' would be cast aside for a couple of months until it was rediscovered. When he had seen the video of the week half a dozen times, he would drive the cars out of the car park, once again in strict order, and put them back into the box. This game was played after breakfast, after lunch and after dinner, and we developed quite a comforting routine.

Because I was concerned at Will's solitary life, I signed him up for the local playschool. The ladies who helped out there told me that they thought he might be autistic, which I denied vehemently. I laughingly shared their diagnosis with my husband, who joined in my delight. As far as we were concerned, Will just felt that he was more intelligent than all the other kids and that was why he didn't join in their games.

Eventually though, it became obvious that there was something wrong with my son; not because of his repetitive play but because he would fly into tantrums over seemingly silly things and because he didn't speak until he was turned three years old, when he spoke in fully formed and beautifully constructed sentences. At school, despite being super-intelligent, he was disruptive and out of control. Letters and phone calls from disgruntled teachers became a fact of life and, when we spoke to Will about it, he always had what he considered to be a valid reason for his behaviour. Then, when he was nine years old, he was diagnosed as having Asperger's syndrome, a condition on the autistic spectrum.

My reaction surprised even me. Yes, of course I was pleased that we now knew why Will behaved in the way he did but, at the same time, my son now had a label. He wasn't the perfect child with whom I fell in love; he was imperfect, defective and shop-soiled. I was devastated and grief stricken. Of course, he hadn't changed; he was still my much-loved and extremely charming youngest child but it would take me a while to come to that realisation. And I may have got there more quickly had I taken my own advice and examined my feelings in the pages of my journal, but it seemed disloyal to write such things. I wish I hadn't been so stupid because what I have come to understand is that what I was dealing with was loss – the loss of my perfect child.

And the relevance of his painful birth? Research has suggested that one of the predisposing factors in children with Asperger's syndrome is having undergone a traumatic delivery.

The other critical moment in my life when loss of health has been an issue was when, after ten years or so of being afflicted with so many minor disorders that my partner and my friends began to think of me as something of a hypochondriac, I was diagnosed with an auto-immune disease that is both chronic and incurable. Even though the symptoms had been present for many years I found that, in light of the formal diagnosis and subsequent 'label', I needed to re-evaluate my perception of who I was and, for a while at least, the diagnosis caused me more angst than the symptoms themselves.

Transformation

Both of these episodes and the torment they caused were about enforced change and my reaction to that change. Of course, another word for change is transformation and it is my hope that by working with the exercises given here you will move from loss to transformation in a positive, life-affirming way. Receiving news of this nature can be deeply shocking and looking to the future when this happens can be a challenge. Take your time, therefore, and allow your journal to help you along the way.

Journaling through loss of health

It can be traumatic to have to deal with the prospect of ill-health. It is difficult to think about not being able to do things that one has taken for granted up to that point, and also to face the prospect of needing some degree of care from other people – most especially for those who are carers themselves or used to independence. Take time to re-adjust and use your journal to help you.

What is my new normal?

Normality is different for different people. For somebody who was born with a disability, restriction of certain activities might seem entirely normal. Rather than thinking how wonderful it would be to get back to normal, it is important for you to realise that how you are now is the new normal. This may be easier said than done but it is a process that can be made much easier by examining your thoughts within the pages of your journal.

In order to address this issue, you could simply do a timed writing using the title 'What is my new normal?' as your prompt. If you would prefer something more structured, you could try writing on the following topics:

✱ Describe the illness in detail.

✱ What problem, if any, does it/will it cause in your life?

❀ Who else will have their normality changed by the diagnosis?

❀ List your fears.

❀ List your solutions.

❀ Write a script for your new life; your new normal.

❀ Write a step-by-step plan for achieving your goals.

Who am I?

This is a really simple exercise. Write a list of positives in your journal, each beginning with the phrase 'I am'. For instance:

❀ I am Dianne.

❀ I am a mother.

❀ I am a wife.

❀ I am a friend.

❀ I am a daughter.

❀ I am a writer.

You will find that your list is almost endless. More importantly, you will also discover that, in reality, the diagnosis doesn't fundamentally change who you are.

Accepting the illness of a loved one

When somebody you love is diagnosed with a chronic or serious illness it may instigate a wealth of unwelcome emotions, some of which may cause you to feel guilty. If you are to help your loved one through this time you need to develop some sort of resilience and coping mechanism for yourself. Explore your feelings and reactions by answering the following questions in your journal. Then, more importantly, act on the answers:

❀ How has this person's illness changed my life?

❀ How do I feel about this illness? You may, for example, feel anger, despair, guilt and resentment.

❅ Write about the feelings you identified in the previous question, for instance, 'I am angry because ...' or 'Despair for me is ...'.

❅ Who will support me whilst I support my loved one?

❅ Why do I feel that person will be able to support me?

❅ How will I ask that person for support?

❅ What positive thing has happened today? It doesn't matter how insignificant this event may seem.

❅ How have I coped with difficulties in the past?

❅ What changes might the illness cause in my life? How will I cope with them?

Expressing the negative feelings

I briefly mentioned above that you may experience some unpleasant feelings, some of which may make you feel guilty. Unfortunately, knowing that these feelings are normal and to be expected won't make them go away. Rather, you need to deal with these negative feelings in a constructive way.

Consider what the following words mean to you in the context of your loved one's illness. You may choose to write about them all or only those that have a resonance to your own situation.

❅ Anger.

❅ Embarrassment.

❅ Shame.

❅ Irritation.

❅ Guilt.

❅ Inadequacy.

❅ Regret.

❅ Worry.

❅ Affair.

❋ Revulsion.

Then, to counter the negative, repeat the same exercise with the following words:

❋ Love.

❋ Enthusiasm.

❋ Triumph.

❋ Honesty.

❋ Devotion.

❋ Friendship.

❋ Birth.

❋ Intimacy.

❋ Loyalty.

❋ Peace.

Emotional Health and Healing

Y ou may think that some of the issues I have included
in this section of the book are more concerned with
mental than emotional health. I find the two things
very difficult to separate and, having turned this over and
over in my mind, I have come to the conclusion that it is all a
matter of degree. Just as in other areas of life, there is a
spectrum of emotional health that ranges from intermittent
feelings of discontent right through to obvious mental health
issues. If somebody is under par emotionally it does not mean
that they are mentally ill, but, as we are beginning to
understand, all of our systems are interconnected: the
physical, the emotional, the spiritual and our thought
processes. At the root of it all, we cannot get away from the
fact that what goes on in the mind has an effect on the rest of
the body.

A recent study at Bristol Royal Infirmary suggested that
writing poetry can significantly improve emotional health,
with 56 per cent of the 200 volunteers stating that their
anxiety levels had dropped whilst they had been involved in
the study, which required them to write poems about their
traumatic experiences. One of the particular benefits of
turning trauma into poetry is seen to be the fashioning of
something beautiful out of pain.

These exercises are designed to help you through various challenges to your emotional well-being and to help keep you emotionally healthy and thus in a better position to withstand the bumps and bruises of everyday life.

As I have pointed out before, if you are suffering from a diagnosed illness, whether mental or physical, these exercises should not take the place of support from a registered health practitioner. There is nothing to stop you journaling alongside whatever other treatment you are receiving but please do discuss it with your psychologist, therapist or general practitioner first.

Journaling for emotional health and healing

Although you will find exercises to help with specific emotional problems at the end of the relevant chapters within this section, there are some exercises that are useful across all spheres of emotional problems. These exercises are shown below.

Food and mood diary

It is well documented and now accepted in traditional medical circles that what you eat has a dramatic effect on both physical and emotional health. Tom, the elder of my two sons, has a medically diagnosed allergy to dairy products, which causes unpleasant physical symptoms if he eats or drinks anything containing milk or its by-products. When the diagnosis was made, we cleared all dairy products from the house so that Tom wouldn't have temptation placed in his way and so that I, in my forgetfulness, wouldn't spread his toast with butter rather than the permitted dairy-free spread.

The removal of these products from the house coincided with a definite change in my husband's personality. He changed from being verbally abusive and very short-tempered to being much more pleasant to be around. He was still prone to flying off the handle unreasonably and we still walked on eggshells for fear of saying something that would provoke his anger but things were definitely better than they had been.

When he was in one of his less aggressive moods I pointed out this change of personality to him and, as a result, he removed all dairy products from his diet outside of the home as well as inside. The result was that the kind, caring man I thought I had married returned.

I am not suggesting that you remove whole food groups from your diet; it would be dangerous to do that without medical support. However, there are proven links between what you eat and problems ranging from anxiety and panic attacks through to depression and behavioural disorders.

In order to assess whether your mood is affected by any of the foods or drinks that you consume, try recording the following information in your journal for a week.

❀ Your mood.

❀ What you eat and drink – including the quantity.

❀ Your feelings before, during and after eating/drinking.

It is obviously better if you can record what you eat as you eat it, but that is not always possible, so before you go to bed is fine, as long as you try not to forget anything.

At end of the week, look at your journal and see if you can find any causative links between food and mood. You may wish to continue the journaling for another week or so to see if any patterns emerge. Be aware that it is quite often the foods you eat on a regular basis that cause the problems.

If you do find a link between your mood and the food you eat, the next step is to contact the relevant organisation listed in the Resources section (see page 184).

Poems from pain

Using the guidelines in Chapter 7 (see page 33), write a short poem of two verses about each of the following negative feelings. For the first verse, concentrate on the negative connotations of the word and then, for the second verse, turn the negatives into positives:

❉ Sadness.

❉ Fear.

❉ Hate.

❉ Pain.

Windows

Imagine you are looking through a window at an aspect of your life. Describe what you see. Try using the following prompts:

❉ You in private.

❉ Your life as a lover.

❉ Your life as an employee.

❉ Your life as a son or daughter.

❉ Your life as a mother or father.

16 *Depression*

As I was researching for this book, I turned up a remarkable statistic: a study of a group of eminent British writers and artists showed that 38 per cent of these people had been treated for mood disorders and that 75 per cent of that group had received medication or in-patient treatment. For me there is a conundrum here – do these people write to escape their demons or is it their demons that cause them to write? I digress, but I do think it's a point worth pondering.

Writing does seem to be an especially effective remedy for depression. James Pennebaker was compelled to begin his research into journaling when he discovered that writing things down helped him to escape the depression into which he sunk as his first marriage ended. From Pennebaker's work and that of other researchers in this field it is clear that not just any old writing will do. The writing has to be about the traumatic and stressful events that have occurred in your life for it to have maximum impact. Blood tests, taken before beginning a spell of writing of this kind and then repeated after several weeks of writing about previously endured emotional pain, have shown that the immune system is strengthened by such exercises. It is not easy to write about painful memories and events but this really is a case of 'no pain, no gain'.

Other positive results seen by researchers were that those who were involved in the studies made fewer trips to their GPs, used less medication, functioned better in day-to-day tasks and scored higher in tests of psychological well-being. Yet another study showed that students who wrote about their anxieties surrounding forthcoming exams were less likely to show signs of depression than other students who were not involved in the writing project.

Why does it work? At this stage I can't find any evidence to suggest that anybody is really sure, but one of the most popular theories is that writing helps us to organise our thought processes. Writing an account of a negative event helps us to archive that event in the brain's filing system. I also believe that you can tell much more to a piece of paper than you can to a psychologist. And you can throw away the piece of paper, or burn it, so that nobody need know what it is you have confided.

Those of us who suffer from repeated periods of depression are thought by cognitive behavioural therapists to indulge in negative thinking, entertaining destructive thoughts, often without realising that we have the tendency. One such thought process involves fortune telling, when we 'know' that something bad will happen. I very clearly remember indulging in this sort of behaviour myself following the birth of my eldest son, Tom.

When Tom was born in 1987 I was convinced that I didn't deserve to have such a beautiful child and that he would be taken from me. I sat outside his room for hours on end in the sure and certain knowledge that if I went into his room I would find him cold and stiff. I simply knew he would die – after all, I had one healthy older child so, in my mind, the odds of losing a child to unexplained infant death were greatly shortened.

At the point of writing, Tom is a handsome six-footer approaching his nineteenth birthday – the nightmare didn't happen. I now know that I was suffering from post-natal depression in the months following his birth, a depression so profound that I viewed life through what appeared to be a long and dark tunnel. This was one of the rare times in my life when I didn't write. Now I wonder if I had written would I have succumbed to the demons? Or, did I succumb to the demons because I wasn't writing? I have no way of knowing but I would have no hesitation in betting that my journey through that tunnel would not have been so long or so dark, had I picked up my pen.

As a midwife I know that one of the worst fears for a new mother is cot death. Often the fear is unspoken but, when I discharge a woman from my care, I make a point of broaching the subject. I believe that bringing the bogeyman out from under the bed and into the sunshine takes away some of his power. Perhaps that is what happens when you write down your fears – you let the light shine into the darkness.

A tendency to get things out of proportion is another trick we depressives tend to play on ourselves – one writer calls it the binocular trick. We see triumphs as smaller than they really are and problems as larger than they really are. I suppose in my cot death phase, I was fortune telling with the use of binoculars!

To eliminate negative thinking completely may be nigh on impossible and, if it is possible, could take a very long time. However, by recognising the destructive thought processes and describing them in your journal you will be well on the way to defusing them and preventing them from destroying your happiness and your life.

The exercises that follow are designed to help you to recognise unhelpful modes of thinking and to defuse them.

Journaling through depression

By definition, it is not always easy to find the energy for writing if you are depressed, so work within your own capabilities and work only in short bursts if that is what is most helpful to you.

Capture your thoughts

At the end of each day undertake a timed writing, for perhaps 15 or 20 minutes, about how you are thinking at the time of writing and how you have thought during the day. When you have finished writing, analyse your thoughts using the following criteria:

* ❈ Are you fortune-telling, that is, have you been jumping to conclusions? For instance, have you assumed that because your partner hasn't said that he loves you today that he has stopped loving you?

* Are you wearing binoculars and getting things out of proportion?

* Are you equating who you are with your mood? Just because you feel fat and ugly doesn't mean you are fat and ugly!

* Have you assumed responsibility for everything that has happened? Not everything is your fault.

* Have you concentrated on the negative and forgotten the positive?

Your perfect day

Describe your perfect day. The following list is just to give you ideas. You could write for hours about this, but I suggest that you do it in 20-minute bursts over a period of a week.

* Where would you wake up?

* Would you be alone or with somebody?

* Who would that person be?

* What would you have for breakfast?

* What would you wear?

* Where would you go?

* What would you do when you got there?

Things haven't always been bad

Write a short piece, approximately 100 words would be adequate, about a happy memory. Describe the memory in detail, concentrating on the smells, sounds, sights and emotions.

Put it in a letter

Write a letter to somebody from the list of suggestions below. In your letter speak about the things that are making you feel depressed and be quite specific about the way you are feeling. For instance, are you feeling sad, lonely, anxious, hurt, betrayed, inadequate or any of the other unpleasant feelings that could come under the umbrella of depression? Some suggestions of who to write to are:

❋ The person you think caused you to feel like this.

❋ Your depression.

❋ Your mother or father.

❋ Your ex-husband or ex-wife.

❋ Your boss.

❋ A school teacher you liked.

❋ God.

17 *Addictions*

What do you see in your mind's eye when you think of an addict: a heroin addict, dead-eyed and wan, craving the next fix; a lonely housewife with a wardrobe full of empty bottles? These are stereotypes at the extreme end of the spectrum of addiction and I would like you to replace those images. For addict, instead of the oversimplified, common concept, think of the young adult who watches television all day, the child who demands another sugary drink or the smart businessman with a desk drawer full of pornography. Or what about the slim young woman who has to be perfect to win approval, the middle-aged mother who is up to the limit on all of her credit cards and the attractive 25 year old who seems to be sick after everything she eats? This is the truth of addiction; it is a compulsion to act in a certain way to detract from the pain of thoughts and feelings.

If you are not an addict there will almost certainly be somebody in your immediate circle who is, even if you are unaware of their problems. In fact, I think that if we look at addictive behaviours as a spectrum, as we did when considering emotional pain in general, and widen the term 'addict' to include compulsion, then every one of us at some stage will probably display some form of addiction. I am aware that the term 'addict' tends to be applied to somebody who is physiologically dependent on a chemical or other substance but, in my personal view, this definition is far too narrow. After all, who is the arbiter of what is simply an unhealthy habit and what is an addiction?

There are many and varied theories about what might lie at the root of a person's susceptibility to addictions and compulsions, ranging from genetics through to an unhappy childhood. One theory, which sounds plausible to me, is that children who have suffered abusive childhoods have not developed sound coping strategies or learned about boundary setting – after all, their own boundaries have been persistently crossed. Another factor I feel must be significant, however, is the amount of peer pressure today's youngsters are under to conform. If all the friends of a 16-year-old boy are drinking alcohol on a regular basis, then there is enormous pressure for the boy to join them. If, in addition to the peer pressure, the child has problems with boundary setting or has issues in his life with which he is having difficulty coping, how likely is it that the boy will become dependent on alcohol?

Enough of theories! How do you know if you're addicted to something? A commonly used assessment tool for alcohol addiction is CAGE but, apart from the 'eye-opener' bit, I'm sure that this device could be applied to other addictive behaviours. Certainly, it would be a start to assessing whether your behaviour is problematic or not.

❈ **C** Have you ever felt that you should **cut** down on your drinking?

❈ **A** Have people **annoyed** you by criticising your drinking?

❈ **G** Have you ever felt bad or **guilty** about your drinking?

❈ **E** Have you ever had an **eye-opener**, that is a drink first thing in the morning to steady your nerves or get rid of a hangover?

Perhaps the most familiar treatment most of us have heard about for helping those with addictions is the Alcoholics Anonymous type management plan, the 12-step programme. I must admit that, until I started researching for this book, I didn't really know what a 12-step programme entailed. Apparently, though, it is based on the premise that those with severe dependencies have lost all control over the use of their drug of choice and the only way forward is complete abstinence. The ensuing abstinence is then policed by the group – hence the emphasis on group meetings.

For me, being told how to act, 'that behaviour is bad, you must not indulge in it and the group will pull you up if you do,' is a complete anathema and I would find that sort of programme very difficult to adhere to. I even get tetchy going to slimming clubs, thinking that what I eat has absolutely nothing to do with anybody else and the group has absolutely no right to pass judgement. The historic success of AA and Weight Watchers proves that, happily, not everybody thinks the same way as me.

When we look at journaling as a method for helping with addiction problems, whether related to shopping for stuff we can't afford and don't need, watching day-time television and forgetting to get dressed, eating too much or mainlining heroin, we are looking at a method that goes in completely the opposite direction to a 12-step programme. Journaling asks us to look inside ourselves for the reasons why we are struggling with addiction. Armed with that knowledge, we are able to apply our own controls.

Once you understand that you create your own feelings you are in a better position to modify those feelings. Does that mean you will be able to get away with moderation rather than abstinence? Unfortunately, I don't think so, depending, of course, on how far down the path to addiction you have travelled and the nature of your drug of choice. If the drug is food or shopping, you have no alternative other than to moderate your behaviour because you can never completely stop eating or shopping. It is for this type of addiction that journaling might best be used.

Journaling through addictive behaviour

Before you can begin to give up whatever it is you are
addicted to, you need to understand exactly what it is you get
from the behaviour or substance you use. You also need to
understand what you are risking by continuing with this
behaviour.

Understanding the problem

Use the following prompts to start the thought processes. How
you write and what you write is up to you; it can be a simple
list or an emotional piece of writing describing exactly what
problems your behaviour is causing in your life. Be honest,
and use your journal as a friend to whom you can reveal your
soul. Try to see beyond the immediate issues and look at the
bigger picture. For instance, your relationship may not be at
risk at the moment but is there a chance that it could be if
you continue your current pattern of behaviour?

* ✿ If I continue behaving in this way, I risk …

* ✿ If I change my behaviour, I risk …

* ✿ The rewards of my addiction are … For example, the
  excitement of buying something new.

* ✿ The rewards of changing are … For example, feelings of
  pride and achievement.

If you work in business or management you will recognise
that this is a basic cost/benefit analysis. If it helps, set it out
as such in your journal rather than using simple lists. See the
Resources section for a template (see page 175).

I eat/drink/shop because …

All of us who indulge in compulsive behaviour have
something that triggers that behaviour; these are known as
activating factors. This next exercise might help you to
identify what your activating factors are, if you don't already
know. If you do know what your factors are, this exercise is
still useful for helping you to address these factors and
change your response. This is best done after you have

indulged in whatever it is you are addicted to. In your journal, write about the following:

* ❧ How did you feel just before you felt the need to eat/drink/shop?

* ❧ What were you thinking just before you indulged your addiction?

* ❧ Try to isolate and write down the sequence of thoughts and feelings before you took the action.

* ❧ What thoughts could you have had instead of the destructive ones?

* ❧ What feelings were you trying to avoid by indulging your addiction?

* ❧ How did you feel after you had succumbed to your addiction?

* ❧ What will you do next time you feel that behaviour coming on?

Trend spotting

Each day, when you get into bed, spend some time writing in your journal about your moods during the day. Has your mood been stable, have you been very changeable, miserable or happy? If you have had a difficult day that has led to you giving in to your addiction, think back to exactly what it was that caused the behaviour.

Over a period of a few weeks or so you should see a trend begin to develop; you will begin to recognise the symptoms that are associated with various moods. Eventually you should be in a position to predict symptoms before they happen and, once you have got to that happy state of affairs, you will be more able to prevent the negative behaviour happening. If you enjoy computer work, why not use a statistics package to plot the trends on a graph or chart? Some of the specifics you could address are:

* ❧ Your cravings – what did you crave and when?

* ❧ Your moods.

❦ Your energy levels.

❦ Your physical health – did you have joint pains, headaches, blocked sinuses or suffer from any other chronic health problem?

❦ Your relationships.

Project management

Once you have identified your triggers and the trends in your situation, the next step is to give yourself some goals. We all do better when we know what we are aiming for and when we hope to achieve it. In management-speak, well-planned goals and objectives are said to be SMART, that is:

❦ **S** Specific   Specify what you want to achieve.

❦ **M** Measurable   Ensure than you can measure your progress.

❦ **A** Achievable   Ensure that your objective is one you can achieve.

❦ **R** Realistic   Ensure that your objective is realistic, given your resources.

❦ **T** Time   Set yourself a deadline.

Using the SMART guidelines write your objectives for dealing with your addiction in your journal. It is important that you are not too optimistic in your objectives. Set yourself small, easily achieved goals so that as you attain them you will feel triumphant and positive; this will help to keep you enthusiastic about your journey. You will find a SMART template in the Resources section (see page 176).

Recovery

The root cause of many problems is negative self-talk and there is no doubt that this is one of the fundamental origins of addictive behaviour. One way to combat this is to exchange some of your negative vocabulary for more positive alternatives. This exercise will be ongoing.

Make a list of some of the negative words and phrases that you use on a regular basis. Now think about different words and phrases you could use instead. For instance, many of us say we are depressed when, in fact, we are just sad. The following is my own negativity list with alternative words just to get you started:

❀ I must ...	I would prefer ...
❀ I can't stand it when ...	I don't like it when ...
❀ I must be the best.	I will try to do my best.
❀ I can't do that.	I would rather not do that.
❀ You always say that.	Sometimes you say that.
❀ I hate my job.	I didn't enjoy work today.

18 *Recovering from Childhood Abuse*

Another small word with enormous meaning: 'abuse' has so many definitions that it may be hard for you to know whether or not your childhood experiences come under this heading. This chapter and the exercises within it are designed to help survivors who have very clear memories of the abuse they suffered as children. In this situation, I am not advocating journaling as a way of uncovering repressed memories. Apart from the controversy surrounding false memory syndrome and the use of guided writing to elicit recollections that are later proved to be false, I believe that trawling for such memories needs to be undertaken in a safe, protected environment and, as an author, I have no control over where my work will be accessed and used.

If you are a survivor of abuse, you may need to use exercises from other chapters in the book; the effects of childhood abuse affect the survivor in a range of situations for the whole of their life. You will note that I haven't sat on the fence here and said that a person 'may' be affected for the rest of their adult life. That is because consequences are certain to occur – there is no maybe about it. As an adult survivor of childhood sexual abuse I have espoused many reasons over the years for some of my physical and emotional issues yet, if I am brutally honest with myself, the effects attributed to survivors mirror almost exactly the problems I have experienced.

The effects of child abuse on the adult survivor

When a trusted person abuses a child, the child is robbed of innocence and security. The childhood is stolen along with a sense of self and an ability to trust others. The surviving adult will endure a degree of emotional pain to equal any physical pain that can be imagined. The only choice the survivor may have is whether to use their experience positively or negatively.

The result of my own experience has been a commitment to help women, both in my job as a midwife and in my social interactions. In fact, my overriding feeling is that out of the ashes of my childhood I have grown into a warm and empathetic adult who shows more understanding and compassion towards people than I otherwise might have done. The other thing that has happened over the years is that I have come to recognise that the perpetrator (in my story anyway) was and is a victim too. This point of view causes heated arguments and serious disagreements with my husband but I feel so strongly that, unusually for me, I refuse to be moved from that viewpoint.

The fact that it is unusual for me to stick to my guns is one of the effects of the abuse, at odds here with another effect – that I am a 'people pleaser', often going out of my way to please others to the detriment of my own well-being.

What follows is an extensive, but by no means complete, list of the effects of sexual abuse of children:

* Alcoholism.

* Drug addiction.

* Self-harming tendencies.

* Prostitution.

* Promiscuity.

* Sexual dysfunction.

* Eating disorders.

❀ Sleeping disorders.

❀ Perfectionism.

❀ Avoidance of intimacy and emotional bonding.

❀ Non-assertiveness.

❀ Problems setting personal boundaries.

Childhood abuse interferes with psychological, emotional and social well-being and the effects are both immediate and lifelong.

Invariably, the victim will shoulder the responsibility for the abuse and mentally minimise what happened in order to preserve the image of their fantasy family and childhood – the life that they think other children were enjoying whilst they existed in their own private hell.

Dealing with the consequences

Look once more at the list of consequences above; you will see that all of the behaviours are self-destructive. Changing them is a long and painful process and I am not suggesting that journaling will be enough to guide you through the whole process, although it can be. I have never had professional help to deal with my own issues, although sometimes I wish I had and I urge you, if you haven't done so already, to access some form of supportive counselling.

In addition to professional help or instead of it, if that is your wish, the exercises here will help you to think deeply about the issues surrounding the events of your childhood. The rewards for being brave enough to address these areas of your life are enormous.

Journaling for survivors of childhood abuse

Communication issues are prominent for survivors because of the constant internal struggle that they experience with their conflicting emotions. Many of their feelings and much of their understanding is distorted, and the secrecy that surrounds such events means that they have very little opportunity to take these feelings out, examine them and redefine them.

Rational Emotive Behaviour Therapy (see Chapter 3, page 16) can make a valuable contribution to abuse issues. As a survivor, it is likely that your experiences will have been denied or trivialised, possibly repeatedly, and this will have led to distortion and negative thought patterns – the very thing that REBT was conceived to address.

Redefine your reality

For this exercise you will need to examine your beliefs using the ABC technique (see page 19). You can either use a photocopy of the template in the Resources section (see page 168) or write straight into your journal. This will be a time-consuming process, possibly taking many months, but as the Chinese proverb says, 'a journey of a thousand miles starts with a single step'.

It is helpful to have a photograph of you as a child in front of you as you do this exercise. If you don't have any photographs of that time in your life, which is a distinct possibility, a picture of any child of around the age you were when the abuse started, will do.

What follows is an example of a distorted thought examined through the ABC technique. In your journal, of course, you could write under each of the headings in much more detail.

❊ A **Activating event**: the abuse.

❊ B **Irrational belief**: I did something to provoke the abuse (for example, I was too sexy and attractive; he had a tough childhood; she was drunk at the time).

❧ **C Consequences**: I feel guilty about what happened.

❧ **D Dispute**: Look at the picture of the child you have in front of you and ask yourself how that child could possibly have provoked any sexual response. How could that child possibly be guilty of provocation?

❧ **E Effective new belief and positive emotional consequences**: A child can never be responsible for being abused. The responsibility lies only with the abuser. It is vital that you don't just do this exercise in your mind because it is the writing down that fixes the new thoughts and ideas in your head.

It is likely that you will have far more than just one damaged view of reality. You should repeat the exercise for all of the distorted views that you are aware you have. It will take a long time and will, at times, be supremely painful, but it will be worth it.

Let it flow

A simple but powerful technique, stream-of-consciousness writing is a method of writing things down while ignoring all formality. There is no punctuation, no need for complete sentences – you simply write what comes into your mind. The writing is uninterrupted and unedited. The only rule is that there are no rules. The act of tidying up our writing as we write also tidies up our thoughts and that, of course, acts as a censor.

Set a timer for ten minutes and write on one of the following:

❧ The person I would like to tell about the abuse is (insert the name of your choice here) and what I would like to say is …

❧ If my abuser were here with me right now, I would say …

❧ My feelings surrounding my abuser are …

❧ My feelings about the abuse are …

It was in this place

In your journal draw a simple ground plan of the place where the abuse took place. If it was at home, draw a map of your home. As you label the rooms within this place you will find that memories will rise to the surface of your mind. Do not censor the memories, but write about them in the stream-of-consciousness style described on page 109.

Write a letter to your abuser

This is a traditional but powerful exercise. Write a letter to your abuser and honestly express your thoughts within it – no holds barred. Describe your confusion between love and mistrust, your inner turmoil and the endless consequences of what happened in your life. It is up to you whether you send the letter or not.

Speak to your inner child

This may sound like therapists' jargon, but as survivors of child abuse, we are quite often stuck at the age that the abuse happened. Because we have to function in the real world of grown-ups, however, we bury that child deep within us and acquire a veneer of adulthood. Over the years, you begin to believe in your own façade and the child gets buried deeper and deeper beneath the acquired veneer. The child is still there, though, and is still a frightened and confused little person.

Making contact with that child within is a very powerful exercise. It's not easy at first and an adult's initial reaction is often to deny that the child exists at all. What worked for me was to go back in my mind to the time of the abuse and remember how I felt and what my thoughts were at that time. I recalled what I was saying to myself inside my head, my internal dialogue.

My own inner voice of the time is far too personal to share within the pages of a book and I have only ever shared it with my journal but I can remember it very clearly, together with the awful duality I felt. I loved my abuser very much indeed, and still do, but I hated what that person became at the times when I was being abused. At the same time, I remember feeling very protective towards the person and wanting to save them from themselves. From my adult perspective, it horrifies me that the child I was had to learn about the subtext of love, hate and fear so early on but, at the time, I just got on with it.

Another way of contacting the inner child is to imagine yourself as a child. Picture yourself at the time of the abuse then, to lessen the impact of this first meeting, place the child that is you behind a glass screen. You can see her clearly and, if you listen really hard, you can hear her voice. Eventually you will be able to shrink the screen and then remove it altogether, at which time you will hear her voice distinctly and be able to feel her feelings.

However you choose to renew your acquaintance with this little person, your next step is to write to her. Ask how she feels about what is happening in her life (for her it is happening right now), how she is dealing with it and what you can do to help her. Listen to her responses very closely and write them in your journal.

Some experts recommend that you write with your left and right hand alternately as you carry out this dialogue. Your dominant hand is used to represent your voice, and you write your questions to the child with this hand. You write her responses with your non-dominant hand. Personally, swapping hands meant that I couldn't keep up with what my inner child was saying to me and I did it all with my dominant hand, but you may find that this method works for you.

If you think this all sounds a bit silly, as I initially did, I would urge you to put your reservations to one side. This is one of the most powerful exercises I have ever done. It was traumatic listening to the child-me talk about her pain, and I felt like I was being turned inside out. But it worked.

19 Eating Disorders

It all starts so innocently, you see the stick-thin celebrities and models in magazines and on the television and think to yourself that, if you lost just a few pounds, your life would be as exciting as theirs. Or, when you look in the mirror, you see yourself as fat and ugly when, in reality, you are neither of those things.

The world in which we live seems to equate thinness with success. Our televisions beam images into our homes of women who are unnaturally thin. The thing is, because we see these images so often, we forget that they are unnatural and start to perceive them as normal.

There is no doubt that excessive weight has an adverse effect on health and that loss of that extra poundage can lead to a longer and healthier life. Spurred on by our medical advisors and by the media, we attempt to lose the excess in an attempt to improve our health and our looks. Sometimes though, we go too far and fail to realise when we cross the line between eating a healthy diet and an eating disorder. Going on a diet doesn't constitute an eating disorder but continuing to restrict food intake despite being a healthy weight does, especially when the food intake is so restricted as to cause health problems of its own.

As I sit here writing these words I feel uncomfortable and ashamed of myself because I am four stone heavier than is healthy for my height and frame. But no matter how hard I try or how ashamed of myself I feel, I cannot seem to eat healthily. I sneak downstairs in the middle of the night and raid the fridge, I open the fridge every time I pass and find something to eat and, when I'm feeling really sad and ashamed of myself, I go on special shopping excursions to the supermarket where I buy a carrier bag full of food, which I subsequently eat. When I'm red eyed and sobbing about how uncomfortable and unattractive I feel, my husband is incapable of understanding why I don't 'do something about it'. I do understand my deeper issues but, unfortunately, sometimes understanding an issue doesn't make it go away.

The main eating disorders are Bulimia Nervosa and Anorexia Nervosa. Currently there are moves afoot to get binge eating recognised as an official disorder – binge eating being like bulimia but without the vomiting and purging.

Journaling is an extremely valuable tool for those who suffer from eating disorders as their thought processes have a tendency to be chaotic. The use of a journal can help the sufferer to recognise negative thought processes and revise them so that they become positive.

Journaling through eating disorders

There are a number of journaling techniques you can use to help you combat these problems.

Count your blessings

This is a simple exercise, but one that is ongoing. Every day in your journal, write about five things in your life for which you are grateful and the reason for your gratitude. The purpose of this exercise is to change your outlook from negative to positive.

Clustering

This is another name for mind mapping. If you like to keep your journal neat and tidy, you'd be better doing this on a separate sheet of paper, though it is worth noting that an untidy journal is often more successful than a tidy one. If your writing, thoughts and ideas are all over the place rather than linear, this method can often allow you to see associations that you wouldn't notice under normal circumstances.

In the centre of your page write the word 'Food' and draw a circle around it; the word you have written will cause many other words to spring into your mind. You should write these words down on the page, joining them to the central word with a line. You will end up with many subsets of ideas sprouting from the main idea. You may be surprised by the words that come out, but don't censor any of them. See the Resources section (page 177) for an example of a clustering diagram.

Clustering is valuable on its own and also as a starting point for further journaling. Extend this exercise by doing timed writings on some or all of the words and ideas that were generated.

I think, therefore I eat

If your pattern of eating is dysfunctional, use this exercise to enable you to see the link between certain moods and what and how you eat. Answer the following questions about your eating in your journal:

* What were your thoughts and emotions before you ate, whilst you were eating and when you had finished eating?

* What were your physical sensations before, during and after eating?

* What did you do while eating? Did you indulge in a ritual?

* What did you eat? Where did you eat it? How did you eat it?

* How could you modify this next time? Could you eliminate part of the ritual?

* How could you substitute a different activity for the eating? Describe what the activity would be and how you would undertake it. Be as detailed and specific as you can.

Track your goals and achievements

If you have a nutrition plan that has been prescribed by a professional or that you are trying to follow in a self-help programme, write the following:

- ❀ The goal of the plan.
- ❀ How you plan to achieve your goal.
- ❀ Triumphs along the way.
- ❀ Disappointments along the way and the circumstances surrounding them.
- ❀ Your thoughts about your goal and the steps you are taking in order to achieve it.

I am strong

Make a list of your gifts and talents, such as compassion, thoughtfulness, writing ability, musical ability. Do not include anything to do with physical appearance.

Back to school

This is one for those of you who enjoy research and academic work. Write an essay about the 'skinny is successful' environment in which we live and raise our children. If you really like academic work, you could write a debate in which you argue for both sides. For the first part of the essay argue in favour of skinniness and in the second part of the essay, argue against skinniness. You might gain some useful insights about your beliefs.

Quick food

If you are to regain a healthy attitude to eating it is essential that you eat regularly and don't miss meals. It will help you to do this if you have food in the house that doesn't need preparation. Make a list in your journal of suitable foods and use it as if it were a shopping list.

20 *Stress*

We all think we know what stress is; after all, we have all been there. Stress, however, has many different definitions and just as many manifestations. My own, very simple, definition is that stress happens when things get too much for you. Perhaps it is our use (or misuse) of language that causes the confusion surrounding stress. Maybe what we are really discussing is chronic stress or distress: the negative physiological and emotional response when stress is intense and unresolved.

Not all stress is bad. Stress is a term used to describe our response to the environment, how we are stimulated by the things that surround us. Without a certain amount of stress we would not be able to function – we would fail to recognise danger, we would not become sexually aroused, we would never learn.

The causes of stress

There are a number of potential stress triggers including changes in our lives, interpersonal issues and social systems. It is when one or more of the sources of stress interact with an individual's personality traits that chronic stress, or distress, may occur.

It naturally follows, then, that certain life events can trigger higher than usual levels of stress and this has been recognised by health professionals for many years. For this reason, a number of stress measurement tools have been developed, one of which, the Holmes-Rahe social readjustment rating scale, is included in the Resources section (see page 178).

It is important to recognise that not all of the events listed in the scale are 'bad'; occasions such as marriage, marital reconciliation and outstanding personal achievements attract not insignificant stress scores. What the majority of the stressors have in common is that they are apt to induce in us a feeling of lack of control, causing us to perceive the situations as threatening, no matter how pleasant they may be. Whilst we may not be physically threatened we may sense threats to our social standing, our popularity, our career or our spiritual or religious beliefs. These threats trigger our fight-or-flight response as readily as any physical threat and the resulting flood of adrenaline causes us to become anxious, irritable and excitable and, because we are so focussed on survival, we may lack concentration and become accident prone.

Physical responses to stress include increased heart rate and blood pressure, which can lead to headaches or, more seriously, a heart attack or stroke. Alternatively or additionally, your immune system is affected, making you more susceptible to any bugs or viruses – which of course, in turn, leads to increased stress. If you have suffered from chronic stress for some time, you may find that your digestive processes are affected, leading to a predisposition to heartburn, constipation, cramping and bloating. You may also become inclined to skin problems, sexual problems, weight loss or gain, and insomnia or chronic fatigue. On a psychological level, an inability to juggle all of the worries and anxieties brought about by the symptoms above, may well lead to depression.

If this sounds familiar to you, then I hope that the exercises in this chapter may be of some help. You will find that writing about your day will assist you in containing your feelings and responses, and controlling your thought processes.

In my own journal I identified my response to times of stress. My mind races, as does my heart and I am left incapable of rational thought or action. One entry reads, 'surely it's not just me whose mind fires off in all directions at once whilst I just sit and watch from the sidelines'. This is a clear example of the fight-or-flight syndrome, when a surge of adrenaline causes my mind to race and leaves me as a helpless bystander.

117

Recognising your stressors

If something sets off your body's fight-or-flight reaction, that
something is a stressor. We have already discussed the fact
that life-changing events can cause stress but it is also
important to realise that, for some of us, it isn't only the
significant episodes in life that can be stressful.

The school run or the journey to work makes an enormous
contribution to the nervous tension in some people's lives. In
the normal course of things, arguments with husbands or
partners, whilst unpleasant for all concerned, should not be
life-changing or lead to the divorce courts, yet when I first
married my husband I was convinced that every argument, no
matter how trivial, would lead to the end of the relationship.
The feelings may have been unfounded but they were very
real and caused me no end of distress. Not all of us react to
the events of life in the same manner; something that causes
me no concern whatsoever may well be extremely nerve-
wracking for you.

When psychologists realised that some of us were more
prone to stress than others, they formulated a definition of A
and B personality types. If you have a low stress threshold
you probably worry about fairly trivial matters (although, of
course, they will not seem trivial to you). Somebody with a
high stress threshold may only start worrying when facing a
major life event, for instance, if they are moving home or
getting married.

What the psychologists realised was that the stress
threshold group you fall into can be predicted by certain
personal characteristics. If you share the characteristics of
those in Group A you will be far more likely to suffer stress
than a person who shares the characteristics of Group B.
Generally, a Type A will try to do several things at one time,
will find it difficult to relax, will speak quickly, and is
obsessed with deadlines. Type B is altogether a more relaxed
personality.

Theories abound in this area. There's the one that says it's
all to do with our childhood and how we were brought up,
and another that states we are genetically programmed to

behave in a certain manner; if you are unlucky enough to have inherited the anger gene you will be particularly prone to stress and its related illnesses. Yet another theory maintains that the mental state of the mother whilst pregnant can have an effect on the baby in the womb. This theory argues that if a mother is stressed during her pregnancy, the child she bears will have a lifelong tendency to experience emotional problems. As a midwife, I am intrigued to know just how many women or, more realistically, how few women complete pregnancy without encountering a certain amount of stress.

If we think about stress within the framework of Rational Emotive Behaviour Therapy we will need to take into consideration the fact that neither people nor circumstances have the power to upset us. What causes our angst is our reaction to the person or event; the cause is our activating event (the 'A' of our ABC). Physically, I suppose, we are at the mercy of life itself but emotional pain is invariably self-inflicted (see Chapter 3, page 16). This may all sound very simplistic, particularly if your partner of 20 years has just walked out of the door. But if you think about it, there is no universal law that says you must feel as you do because of what has happened. You need to examine why you feel like this. What is the thought process that led to this emotional pain? How can you address these feelings and therefore begin to heal the pain?

This is, of course, quite an extreme example and, if your partner has just left you, I imagine that you will be suffering far more than everyday stress. Although REBT is a valid technique to help you to deal with your pain, at this point in time you will probably be better served by using some of the exercises in the Loss, Change and Grief section of this book (see pages 43–88).

Are you stressed?

The following are all common symptoms of being overstressed although, of course, you can exhibit these symptoms for other reasons. Look through the list and see if any apply to you. If they do, your first step is to make an appointment and see your family doctor to eliminate any more serious cause. Once you are sure the symptoms are stress related, turn to the next exercise to address them through journaling.

* ❋ Anti-social feelings
* ❋ Breathlessness.
* ❋ Excess tiredness.
* ❋ Headaches.
* ❋ Inability to sleep.
* ❋ Indigestion.
* ❋ Indulgence in addictive behaviours.
* ❋ Lack of sexual interest.
* ❋ Loss of appetite.
* ❋ Nausea.
* ❋ Overeating.
* ❋ Palpitations.
* ❋ Restlessness.
* ❋ Road rage.
* ❋ Skin irritations.
* ❋ Vague aches and pains.

Journaling for stress reduction

One of the most important things to remember here is that you are using these exercises to help you reduce your stress levels, so it is important to try the option to which you are initially attracted and not worry about whether it is the right one. You can always try something else if you find your choice doesn't suit your mood.

Pick up your pen

Consider each of your stress symptoms in turn over the course of the next week and write for ten minutes in your journal about each of them. How and what you write is up to you but, using headaches as one of the more common symptoms, the following is an example of how you might address them in your journal.

* ❀ Chronicle the history of your headaches. How old were you when they started, etc?

* ❀ Can you remember a particular time in your life when they were worse or better?

* ❀ List and describe any particular warning signs or symptoms for your headaches.

* ❀ If you treat your headaches differently on different occasions, using a variety of medication or self-help techniques, for example, document these and write down the effects. This will be ongoing until you have learned to manage your headaches.

* ❀ If you can bear it, whilst you have a headache, write about it in as much detail as you can.

I did this exercise one evening when I felt particularly wretched. No medication had worked and I couldn't find a comfortable place to put my head. Then I remembered somebody saying to me many years ago that I should go with the pain, let it wash over me and not fight it off. On this occasion I combined that advice with journaling, and the detail I got was astounding. Amongst other things, I described the pain as egg shaped, with the narrow end of the egg pressing through my spinal cord as if it were trying to take away my mobility and prevent me from doing anything. When I felt better, I wrote for some time about that idea and got some very useful insights. It is certainly worth a try.

Keep a stress diary

Although you might view this as just another 'To do' to add to your list, if you can find the time, you will reap the rewards quite quickly. It's a very simple exercise but it has to be done on a regular basis to be effective. Ideally you should write in your journal throughout the day, timing your entries in order to help in analysing the data later. Failing that, write as often as you can on the following topics:

* Describe your mood.

* Rate your happiness quotient on a scale of 1 to 5, with 1 equalling thoroughly miserable and 5 equalling ecstatically happy.

* Do the same thing with how stressed you feel, with 1 equalling extremely relaxed and 5 equalling extremely stressed.

* If you are stressed, describe your physical symptoms.

* Record the event that triggered your stress.

* Did you attempt to defuse the event? If you did, how did you feel when it was successful/unsuccessful?

* How would you deal with the trigger episode if it happened again?

With this journaling exercise it is vital that you review your entries after a period of a week or two when you should be able to see a pattern in your stress levels and be able to identify the events, people or places that cause you stress.

Shoot down your triggers

Once you have identified your triggers by keeping a stress diary, write about them in your journal. For instance, if a particular person is causing you stress, you could write as follows:

* What is it about x that makes me feel stressed?

* What is it about me that causes x to make me feel stressed?

* How can I change my thinking about x?

* How do I react now to x?

* How I will act in the future? (Notice I've used the word 'act' rather than 'react'.)

ABC

Using the ABC process as described in Chapter 3 (see page 19) and using the template provided in the Resources section if you wish (see page 168), analyse your reaction to the triggers you have identified.

Pleasures

The purpose of this exercise is to help you rediscover some sort of balance in your life because even whilst you are in the midst of stressful situations there is still pleasure to be had. The sort of pleasures I have in mind are those that are free or that cost very little, things like watching a sunset, watching a weepy movie with a friend, feeling your child's hands around your neck. If you start writing about costly pleasures – new perfume, new clothes or a holiday – you are likely to start stressing about money!

* Compile a list of things that give you pleasure.

* Write about them and why they give you pleasure.

* When was the last time you indulged in one of these pleasures? Write about it, paying great attention to your sensory perceptions. What could you see, hear, feel, taste and smell? Relive the memory as profoundly as you possibly can.

Celebrate your achievements

Very simple and very powerful, this exercise appeals to our need for completion as well as our need to recognise our triumphs. Make yourself a list of things you want to achieve, putting the simplest first. Then set out to complete each task and tick it off your list as you do so. The sense of achievement generated by ticking things off your list is a wonderful stress buster.

21 *Anger Management*

The most important point in this chapter is that it's okay to be angry. In fact, some anger is positively healthy. Once you understand that, you will be in a better position to manage both your anger and the way it makes you feel. This may sound like a contradiction, and you may be asking why you should manage something that is not only okay but also healthy. To answer that question we need to understand what anger actually is and why, sometimes, it can degenerate into feelings that are far from helpful in our dealings with others.

Maybe it's just me, but I think we live in a very angry world today. I grew up in the 1950s and 1960s that, in retrospect (and possibly through rose-tinted glasses), seemed to be a much gentler time. Today we are bombarded with information about protecting our rights; consider, for example, those advertisements on daytime television offering no-win no-fee compensation. It's as if somebody always has to be blamed when something goes wrong. Yet none of us gets out of bed in the morning thinking 'I'm going to make a mistake today and, what's more, that mistake will have a detrimental effect on somebody else's life.' To my mind, blaming is just another expression of anger.

Anger is a very simple word that we use to cover a whole gamut of emotions; a quick check in a thesaurus for synonyms gives us annoyance, rage, irritation, fury and resentment. Anger is what is known as a natural adaptive response: that is, if we are threatened, our feelings of anger will ensure that we take any necessary protective action. Unfortunately the natural and instinctive response is aggression, which might have been useful in ancient times but which can get us into a whole load of trouble now. And there is the nub of the problem – aggression is not to be tolerated but it is a natural response to feeling threatened.

We may use a variety of responses to feelings of anger that can be roughly subdivided into three categories: we can express our anger, which can be healthy; suppress our anger, which is unhealthy; or we can take measures to calm the feelings inside – which is where journaling comes in. Obviously, when somebody or something riles you, you can't get out your pen and paper – even if the pen is mightier than the sword. Just write it all down as soon as you can to prevent the unexpressed anger from boiling over and being taken out on innocent people.

The exercise in this chapter is based on the theories of Neurolinguistic Programming (NLP), which, in simple terms, attempts to provide an instruction manual for using your brain. We get instruction manuals with cookers, cars, televisions, computers and practically everything else that we use in our daily lives; our brain, however, the most sophisticated computer known to man, comes with no instructions whatsoever. The premise of NLP is that we need to learn how to use our brains in order to be the best we can.

When I learned to be a midwife, I was allocated to a mentor, an expert practitioner. This person provided me with a clinical model of care that I initially copied and later, when I was more experienced, modified to suit my own needs. By that time, I understood why I was doing things and didn't just do them because that was the way I had been shown. To be an expert practitioner, it is not the 'doing' that is important but the insight into the processes that underlie the doing: the thought processes, underlying beliefs and decision-making processes. So it is with NLP.

NLP studies the structure of thought and experience in people who excel at whatever it is they do. The trick then is to adopt these thought processes and behaviour so that you too can excel. It is a very difficult therapy to explain without using jargon but if you want to make a more in-depth study, refer to the Bibliography (see page 186).

Journaling to understand and manage your anger

If our method of dealing with a situation is not working, then we need to try to find an alternative, and the more flexible we are in our responses the more successful we will be at dealing with life issues. This exercise is, in reality, a series of exercises that should keep you journaling for a month or so.

Part 1: Finding your anger triggers

Once a trigger has been activated your feelings will go on 'automatic pilot'. That is, there will be inevitability about it all because of the way your mind has been programmed over the years. It makes sense, therefore, to learn to recognise your triggers.

For the next week or so concentrate on the aggravations of your day and gradually build a list of what it is that irritates you. The best way to do this is to carry a small notebook with you so that you can write down the trigger as it occurs. If you feel a bit self-conscious about this, try using an index card or a scrap of paper. The point is that you document it as it occurs, because you will be inclined to forget if you leave it until later on.

Part 2: Scoring your anger triggers

Within a couple of weeks you should have compiled quite a good list of the things that irritate you, some of which you may find surprising. The other thing you will have discovered is that your anger can vary in scale from mild irritation to downright uncontrollable fury. With this in mind, go back through the previous exercise, rating your anger at each event on a scale of 1 to 10, with 1 being mild irritation and 10 being the uncontrollable fury that, hopefully, you don't experience very often.

In your journal make two columns and, in the first, write a list of your triggers, starting with the thing that causes you most anger and stress, working down in intensity.

In the second column, next to each trigger, write down the feelings that it invoked in you. For instance, if we consider the irritation I sometimes feel at incessantly moaning colleagues, one of the feelings I would write is 'inadequacy', because the moaning always makes me feel that it is up to me to do something about it. Remember that there may be more than one feeling and that you should list them all.

Part 3: Managing your anger triggers

Now that you have gained some insight into some of the things that rub you up the wrong way, it's time to start reprogramming your brain.

Choose one of the triggers from your list and write it as a heading on a page in your journal. Beneath the heading write your usual interpretations and reactions in such situations. For instance, if the trigger you are exploring is 'my husband sulks', your usual interpretations and reactions might go along the lines of 'I hate it when he does that. Why can't he tell me what's wrong? What have I done to upset him now?'

When you've done that, write down the ramifications of your usual reaction. For instance, an example from my own journal, concerning my husband, who is inclined to sulk: 'I worry for days about what it is I've done to upset him and I probably haven't done anything at all. He might not even be sulking, he might be brooding on a problem at work or he may be feeling under the weather. But I keep on badgering him. Then he gets angry and we have a row.'

Finally, on the opposite (or next) page, write down better ways of dealing with this situation than becoming angry. For instance, I could choose to accept that this is the way my husband has always behaved, or I could try to encourage him to talk about whatever it is that is bothering him.

To incorporate what you have learned into your life and build upon it, you may like to write the trigger on an index card with your better ways of dealing with it written on the back. Carry the card with you for a week or two. When the trigger is activated, tell yourself that you are no longer a victim when this situation occurs and remember the better way of dealing with it. You could perhaps carry a different card each week, which would eventually help you to address all of your identified stressors. The resulting stress relief has got to be worth the small investment in time.

Physical Health

I was so excited when I read of the research that suggests journaling is not only an emotional balm but can help improve physical symptoms as well. The most prolific researcher on this subject is Professor James Pennebaker, head of the Psychology Department at the University of Texas.

Together with his students he has been researching the links between writing and health since 1997. They have discovered that physical health and work performance are significantly improved by simple writing and talking exercises; more specifically, people who wrote about traumatic life experiences had a greater improvement in health than those who wrote about day-to-day experiences. The research is in a relatively early phase and still ongoing but has already proved what many instinctively knew – that our emotions and our reactions to them play a large part in determining our physical health.

Because this is such a new area of research, there are not quite so many exercises in this section compared to the others, but they are still worth doing. Even if you don't suffer from one of the chronic diseases referred to, the journaling work suggested here will help you on the path to a deep self-knowledge. With the scientific proof that writing can help you overcome the ravages of physical as well as emotional ill-health, can you afford not to do these powerful, simple and inexpensive exercises?

22 Keeping a Wellness Journal

As with other areas that you might address through journaling, it is not essential to keep a specific journal dealing with physical ill health. However, you might find it useful both in terms of the emotional trauma that you inevitably experience during a chronic illness and as an illness management tool.

If you decide to keep a journal as an aid to managing your illness, perhaps the first thing to be done is to think of a positive name for it. Pennebaker's research proved quite conclusively that the more positive the language a person uses, both in speaking and writing, the more improvement they can expect to see in their health status. If you call your tool an 'illness management journal', the first word that jumps out at you is illness. Hence the choice of title for this chapter.

What should you think about including in your special journal? My suggestions follow, but do remember that they are only suggestions and are offered as a basis for personalisation.

* Contact numbers for health professionals involved in your care.

* An up-to-date list of medication you take, together with times and dosages and any side effects. (See the Resources section, page 180, for a medication chart.)

* Instructions to be followed if you are taken ill and are not able to explain about your illness and your management of it. For instance, if any of your medications or their routes of administration are unconventional, be sure you include the directions, otherwise the traditional route of administration will be used by the health professionals.

❀ Any booked appointments you may have.

❀ The efficacy of the various medications you take.

❀ Any side effects you have noticed from medication.

❀ How you deal with your illness on a daily basis.

❀ Any interesting information about new treatment breakthroughs.

❀ Anything you would be embarrassed to tell a stranger but which they might need to know in order to help you. In this situation, you can just direct them to the correct page in your journal.

❀ Your feelings when you received the initial diagnosis.

❀ Emotions surrounding your illness.

❀ Hopes and fears surrounding your illness.

❀ How you view your future and what impact the illness may have.

❀ Any pessimistic thoughts that may plague you.

It is entirely up to you how revealing you are about your emotions within this particular journal as it might not necessarily be private. Because of its illness management application, it may be taken with you when you see various health professionals or if you become an inpatient. Certainly, if you have dealings with people who you feel would manipulate you on the basis of what you have written it would be better to keep the soul-searching material completely separate.

23 *Auto-immune Diseases*

If you are suffering from an auto-immune disease, the chances are that it took you years to get a diagnosis. These diseases are good mimics and frequently masquerade as other, more common ailments. The journey to diagnosis can lead to feelings of frustration, anger and despair. Finally, when the correct diagnosis has been made, people often feel cheated out of the years when they felt poorly but did not know the reason why. Whether you are still on the road to diagnosis or have reached the destination and feel cheated and angry, writing your thoughts and emotions in your journal can go a long way to helping you to process the information and integrate it into your life.

When your illness is first diagnosed, the emotional responses may be many and varied and, in order to move forward, you need to come to a deep understanding of why you feel the way you do. Certainly, if you are a person who tends to put a brave face on things, your journal is a place where you can feel free to be yourself. It can be remarkably tiring to keep smiling when all you want to do is cry and bemoan your fate – both of which are perfectly normal responses.

It is vital that you understand your disease, but this group of diseases is so complex that even the medical professionals have difficulty in comprehending them. In the best patient–doctor relationships the learning process becomes a partnership where you learn and progress together. Your doctor should be happy for you to question treatment plans and diagnoses. A true partnership involves contributions from both parties so, if there are any changes in your condition, such as the occurrence of a new symptom, it is important that you tell your doctor about it on your next visit. Your illness journal is the ideal place to record such changes. For some of the auto-immune diseases, medication can be a little hit and miss; if you are prescribed a different medication, record any reactions that you may have to that medication – whether good or bad – so that your regime can be tailored precisely to your needs.

One of the other major issues for sufferers of auto-immune diseases is that often they look perfectly healthy. This means that, when they have to take time off work for sickness they feel almost fraudulent – there may not be many, or indeed any, visible signs of the illness. And in the years before diagnosis, which many sufferers endure, work colleagues may begin to regard the sufferer as a malingerer or hypochondriac. The sufferer knows that there is something wrong but the symptoms may be so non-specific that she too begins to feel that she must be imagining things – or that she is simply lazy.

I hope that some of the exercises that follow will help you deal with these issues, and help you to come to terms emotionally with enduring chronic pain and fatigue, and the feelings of depression that these may bring. If you suffer from any of the following diseases, then I believe that journaling can be of help: fibromyalgia, chronic fatigue syndrome, lupus, multiple sclerosis, Behçet's disease, rheumatoid arthritis and many more.

Journaling through physical illness

Journaling can be very useful in helping you work through issues related to illness. Focus on those points that you find most troubling.

List-making

The simplest way to start journaling your illness is to make lists. You could, for instance, list the following:

* ❋ How my life has changed since diagnosis.
* ❋ How I can manage the illness.
* ❋ How my friends'/partner's perception of me has changed.

❀ The strengths I possess that will help me through.

❀ The positive aspects of the diagnosis.

Letter-writing

This has come up in other sections of the book and I make no apologies for repeating it here. It is one of the most powerful writing exercises you can do. Write letters to any of the following:

❀ The illness.

❀ The pain.

❀ The joints that no longer work.

❀ Your god or the universe.

❀ Your partner.

❀ Your parents.

❀ The medics.

❀ The medication that can sometimes seem worse than the disease.

❀ Your anger.

❀ The tiredness.

You do not need to send these letters and, of course, there is nowhere to send some of them, but the act of writing them will enable you to rant and rave at the universe, open your heart to your mum or thank the medics for their help. All of these things and more will help to give you peace of mind.

Walk a mile in my shoes

The purpose of this piece of writing is to help you to understand how those close to you are feeling. If you have had to support a close friend or family member through a traumatic time in the past, write about how that felt for you, and what your thoughts and fears were. Remember how difficult it was to know what to say or do. This will help you to understand how those who love you feel about your illness.

Collect the words of others

Sometimes we hear a song on the radio or remember a line from a poem that puts into words exactly how we feel. Write down any lyrics, poems or wise words that you find helpful.

Reasons to be cheerful?

Write them in your journal! Make lists of the good things in your life; write about the stunning view from your window or how the sun makes you feel when it shines on your face. Write about the love of your children or your partner. In short, write about things that bring a smile to your face – you will find that smile returning as you write. The best time to do this exercise is when you are feeling particularly miserable. You may have to force yourself to pick up the pen but it will be worth it.

24 Dealing with Terminal Illness

Many of the exercises in this chapter are exactly the same as those in the previous chapter. However, when faced with terminal illness, what one is really dealing with is the inevitability of death. In my admittedly limited experience of these issues, I have found that often it is easier for the person who is dying to accept the inevitable than it is for the people who love and care for that person. As we have already dealt with bereavement, this chapter is specifically targeted at the person who has received the news that they will not recover from this particular illness.

One of the major factors in dealing with the inevitability of your own death is your belief system. My own belief is that dying is just another stage in my life, a life that will continue, albeit in another form, after the dying is done. This belief means that, whilst the process of dying scares me, death itself holds no fears. The first journaling task, therefore, is to write about your belief system.

Even if you are clear in your mind about what you believe, you will still be left with the shock and distress at the diagnosis you have been given. It is one of those things that happen to other people and not to you – and you will need to overcome the initial feeling of complete disbelief. If you have had your symptoms for some time, you may have rehearsed the moment of diagnosis many times in your head but you will still not be prepared for the reality of the words when they are spoken. You will, quite literally, be in receipt of a death sentence.

As with bereavement, a number of emotional phases have been identified as being universal in the process of dying. First there is the disbelief, which is usually accompanied by denial and a need to be alone. This is followed by anger and resentment, and then by attempts at bargaining with God in an effort to avoid the inevitable. Once the reality is acknowledged, which is the next phase, a period of depression is common. Only once all of these phases have been experienced does the person reach a stage of acceptance. Journaling is an ideal tool to use throughout the whole process and can even hasten the onset of the acceptance phase.

Journaling through terminal illness

When I began to write this chapter I felt a frisson of something to which I couldn't put a name, but which I eventually realised was the fear of dealing with a taboo subject. Why should it be taboo? The only certainty in our lives is that we will die. I hope that the following exercises will help you to walk a winding and rocky path with certainty and peace in your soul.

I'm a believer

The purpose of this set of exercises is to understand your belief system. Often we go through life with just a vague perception of our beliefs. We are then brought up short when faced with the reality of our own imminent death or the death of somebody we love. When dealing with the death of my mother I became very confused and began a spiritual search that confused me even more. By writing about your beliefs in your journal you will avoid the panic and confusion that so often comes at this time. The following are only suggestions but they will set you on your own path of discovery:

* ❀ Who is my god and what does he or she look like?

* ❀ Who am I, and what is my purpose in this life?

* ❀ What is the most valuable thing I will leave behind?

* ❀ Where did I come from when I was born?

* ❀ Where will I go when I die?

* ❀ What is the human soul? What shape, colour and weight is it?

If you do these exercises with openness and honesty you will be amazed at the things you discover about yourself.

The wisdom of others

If you find difficulty in beginning to write about such a profound topic, plunder the work of those who have gone before. As long as you are writing for yourself and not for publication, there is no reason why you shouldn't do this. I give two examples below, but you will find many more if you look around you – in books and on the internet. You may already have some lyrics or quotes that move you and that can be used as a starting point.

> When you are sorrowful, look again in your heart and you shall see that, in truth, you are weeping for that which has been your delight.
>
> *Kahlil Gibran*

> When you were born, you cried and the world rejoiced. Live your life so that when you die, the world cries and you rejoice.
>
> *Native American expression*

Timed writings

Write for ten to 20 minutes on the following topics. If you wish, this could be a gift to those you love when you have gone. It will be a singular gift and of enormous emotional and spiritual value to whoever is lucky enough to receive it.

* The things in my life that I am thankful for.

* The things in my life that have scared me.

* An important lesson I have learned that I would like to pass on.

* Advice for younger friends and relatives.

* What I would like to be remembered for.

* How I felt about being a mother/father/sister/ grandmother.

Letters sent and unsent

As before, it is up to you whether you send these letters. Write a letter to:

* ❄ The cancer, or whatever else it is, that is invading your body.

* ❄ Your partner, children, grandchildren or friends.

* ❄ Yourself about how you feel, how you are behaving and why.

* ❄ Yourself, in which you list instructions for how to deal with what is happening to you.

25 Healing through Humour

As I read back through what I have written in the last chapter, some of it seems rather bleak. Chapters on the death of a child or dealing with terminal illness are hardly full of laughs. In reality, however, it is laughter that often helps us to deal with life's catastrophes. And it would seem that this is not just anecdotal or experiential but backed up by medical research.

There is healing in humour, and the physiological study of humour even has its own name: gelotology. I have read reports of cancer patients using humour to help them through their suffering and of the recently bereaved using laughter to help them rise above their grief. In America there is even an Association for Applied and Therapeutic Humour, a non-profit group of health professionals who have realised the therapeutic benefits of laughter, and there is the research to support them in their stance. It has been found, for example, that people who have suffered a heart attack can substantially reduce the chances of suffering a second attack, lower their blood pressure and also decrease their medication by indulging in humour for 30 minutes a day. Conversely, it has also been shown that those suffering heart disease laugh 40 per cent less in a humorous situation than those who are well.

So what exactly are the physiological effects of having a good laugh? Laughter oxygenates the blood because it causes the lungs to expel stale air, allowing more fresh air to enter. It activates the hypothalamus, pituitary and adrenal glands, causing a decrease in the stress hormones adrenalin, noradrenalin and cortisol, and an increase in the secretion of endorphins, our body's natural painkiller. A surge of endorphins can cause a feeling of being 'high' and also causes our muscles to relax as the tension flows from our bodies.

Following a really good belly laugh it can, apparently, take up to two hours for the abdominal muscles to regain their tone. Laughter also causes a rise in the body's immunity due to an increased circulation of immunoglobulins in the blood. And I hear that laughing one hundred times a day gives you as much exercise as ten minutes of rowing. I know which activity I'd prefer.

Sometimes though, in times of tragedy, it can seem inappropriate to laugh. For instance, when I heard my mother was dying with cancer, the last thing I expected to do was laugh. Quite the reverse. As I raced to her side, I told myself that I would not cry, but that I would be brave and try to be strong for her.

Of course, the minute I saw her face I burst into tears. She was lying in bed in acute pain but she told me not to worry and wiped away my tears with a large white cloth. She then offered me the same cloth so that I could blow my nose. On closer examination I saw that the large white cloth was in fact a pair of 'granny' knickers that had seen better days. The waistband elastic was held together with a nappy pin that must have fastened the nappies of my two brothers and me many years previously. In my normal, less than tactful manner I expressed a certain amount of disdain. I will never forget the response of, 'Never mind, darling, your brother used them as well, so you're not the only one.' The ensuing laughter helped us to relax and rediscover ourselves at a time of immense emotional and acute physical pain. Also, it left me with a precious and funny memory of one of the worst times in my life; it was a gift.

What my mother said about the person who had given her a very thick book to read, knowing that the doctors had pronounced that she had only three weeks to live, is unrepeatable but it turned my tears of sadness into tears of laughter and reminded me that the woman dying in the bed was still my mum and not the disease that had claimed her.

Journaling with humour

Unfortunately, if you are going through a very tough time in your life, in the initial period at least, those around you are unlikely to be a bundle of laughs for fear of appearing uncaring or of behaving inappropriately. You have two options: make them laugh just as my mother did for me, or write about the stupid things people say rather than be honest with you, and have a good laugh at their expense. Why not? Nobody need know except you (and your journal, of course).

Laughter is the best medicine

Choose from the following subjects for timed writings:

* ❋ What does the phrase 'laughter is the best medicine' mean to you?

* ❋ Write about a funny experience in your life.

* ❋ Write about the last time you laughed uncontrollably.

* ❋ What colour is humour and why?

* ❋ If you have children or grandchildren, think and write about some of the funny things they have said.

* ❋ Write about a time when something funny happened to someone you love.

* ❋ Imagine that laughter is a person. Describe the person and write a dialogue with him or her.

* ❋ Write about some of the silly things people will do to avoid discussing your situation openly with you. There is a rich vein of humour to be mined in these circumstances.

Other Benefits of Journaling

B eing healthy is not just an absence of physical or emotional malaise; in the definition used within this book, being healthy involves everything that you are being in balance.

In some belief systems a five-pointed star or pentagram is used as a symbol of totality. This ancient symbol does not deserve its sinister reputation, which has grown up partly as a result of its manipulation to represent the devil (by turning it upside down so that it looks like a horned goat).

The Greek philosopher Pythagoras held that the pentagram represented the five-fold division of the body and the human soul. The points of the star were named for fire, air, water, earth and spirit – the ancients believing that these five elements were the basis of all life. My belief is that the modern model of medicine concentrates on the physical – fire, earth, air and water – but forgets the soul, represented in the pentagram as spirit.

We all know of people who, when struck down by some tragedy or other, appear to 'take it on the chin' and get on with life. Likewise, we will know of others who are left prostrate by seemingly insignificant events. This, I think, is where the spirit comes into play.

Journaling is an incredibly powerful tool for healing or strengthening the spirit. The spiritual elements addressed in this section, such as personal growth and self-esteem, have been chosen strictly because working on these areas can have a positive impact on both physical and emotional health. Every one of us feels better within ourselves when we are fulfilling our potential, and these exercises will help you to make a start on building a strong spirit.

26 *Personal Growth*

Why include personal growth in a book about healing? According to a number of commentators in the early to middle part of the twentieth century, in order for an individual to be totally healthy he needs to achieve his full potential. Not to do so can, they postulate, lead to poor physical and emotional health. I think that many of us know this as fact without the need to understand the science behind it. That feeling of 'there has to be more to life than this' doesn't predispose us to feel full of health and vigour.

It may be that, whilst you are not suffering from any particular trauma or illness, you have a sense of just going through the motions in your life; sure that there must be more than this but not sure how or where to find the 'more'. My definition of personal growth is striving to fulfil your potential, striving to be all that you can be and, in the process, reaching the maximum physical and emotional health that is possible for you.

Personal growth is, I think, an umbrella term that covers many aspects, such as improving self-esteem, spiritual development, having better relationships, performing better at work. What these all have in common are the need to expand one's thinking and horizons; the need to set goals and then work out how to achieve them. Your goals and how you achieve them are the focus of this chapter.

This may sound simple but, of course, there is no 'one size fits all' when it comes to the definition of personal success. We all have different strengths and weaknesses, likes and dislikes, needs and desires. Your goals won't be my goals and my goals are totally different to those of my friends. This sounds obvious but I believe that a lot of distress is caused by people striving for something that they do not really want, in the mistaken belief that they *should* want whatever it is. They will then either become miserable in the striving or, when the goal is finally achieved, be unhappy with what they have attained.

Rule number one then is to recognise who you truly are and what it is that would make you feel happy and successful in your life. I have strived for many years to be in a position of authority at work as proof, I suppose, that I am valuable, worthy and clever. Now that I have achieved my aim, I really hate it! I didn't recognise that my love was the day-to-day communication and support of women until it was too late. Strangely, or perhaps not, since I have been in my current post I have struggled with both physical and emotional health problems. I believe there is a message here for us all.

It is all very well for me to exhort you to 'know thyself' but in a world where it is difficult to isolate exactly what it is you really need, it is far from simple to acquire that self-knowledge. One of my heroes is Carl Jung who identified a process he called individuation, a progression towards a conscious realisation of who you really are. He identified the 'you' of the subconscious as being separate from the superficial 'you' that you present to the world. Concentrating on development of the outward 'you' takes you further and further away from the genuine 'you'. That is, in effect, what happened to me with regards to my career.

There are various ways to analyse your personality type. You may be familiar with the personality profiles and psychometric testing often used during the recruitment process. One of the most popular of these tests is the Myers Briggs Type Indicator (MBTI)®, which is based on the work of Jung and his identification of what he called the four functions. Thinking and Feeling he labelled as the rational functions, whilst Sensing and Intuition were the irrational functions. Jung argued that your functional expression, together with whether you were extrovert or introvert, defined your personality type. MBTI® developed this thinking into a system that identifies 16 personality types.

There are many other theories and tests, all of which go way beyond the scope of this book. If you are interested in learning more, see the Personal Growth section of the Bibliography (see page 189).

I believe that journaling can be an effective tool for finding out who you really are, and the following exercises should help you along that path.

Journaling towards self-knowledge

Some methods of examining your personality involve ticking boxes and then analysing what the ticks say about you. This is not an easy option, however, and only categorises you, putting you in a particular box with those people who have answered the questions in the same way. The following exercises are more challenging, do not categorise you and go further towards a personal journey of self-discovery.

Remembering pain

Events from our past inform the 'self' we now are, often subconsciously. The purpose of writing about the following topics is to uncover residual fears and pain that may be preventing you from achieving your full potential.

- Write about the worst time in your life, a time that changed your life forever. Relive the event physically and emotionally.
- Using the event above, imagine that at that time you had been in possession of the knowledge you have now. Using that knowledge, try to solve the problem and identify the lesson to be learned.
- Write a letter from who you are today to the person you were in the event you have written about. What wisdom can you pass on?
- Write a timed piece of ten to 20 minutes for each of the following topics. Actually start your piece with the phrase given:
  - It was me who …

* I have learned ...

* I wish I had ...

* I wish I had not ...

Remembering pleasure

We are not only a result of the bad stuff that has happened to us but also of the good stuff. If we are in receipt of praise and admiration for something we have done well, it is likely that we will continue to do that thing. We all like to be seen as being good at something. Focus on the positive and write about some of the following subjects:

❋ The best days of your life.

❋ A time in your life when you felt at ease with yourself, when you felt free to be who you really are.

❋ A time when you were true to yourself and told the truth in a difficult situation. Remember the feelings associated with speaking out.

❋ In the previous set of exercises you wrote from your wiser and older self to a younger you who was going through a traumatic time. Now, reverse that, and write a letter from a younger and more spontaneous you to the older and wiser you.

❋ Write a timed piece of ten to 20 minutes for each of the following topics. Actually start your piece with the phrase given:

* I'm really good at ...

* My favourite place as a child was ...

* I'm glad I ...

* Things I loved as a child ...

* When I believed in Father Christmas ...

I am

That you are unique is not in doubt, neither is it in doubt that you are good at some things and not so good at others. Here are some exercises to make you think deeply about who you are. If you don't know who you are, how is anybody else supposed to know?

❀ Write a timed piece of ten to 20 minutes for each of the following topics. Actually start your piece with the phrase given:

  * I see myself as ...

  * I would like to be remembered for ...

  * I am different because ...

  * I think heaven is ...

  * I think hell is ...

Fantasy

This piece of writing, with no time limit, is designed to uncover the real you. Imagine you have been granted the opportunity to live whatever life you want – no holds barred. There are no musts and there are no must nots, and you should write from the perspective of your soul, forgetting about your current life and the restrictions placed upon you by the responsibilities that you have. Describe this life as fully as you can. Think about your surroundings, your friends, your lovers and your emotions. Really go for it and, in your imagination, do whatever it is you really want to do.

27 Self-esteem

I'm sure that everybody from time to time thinks that, in the general scheme of things, they are useless at everything. For a person with a healthy level of self-esteem this is just one of the ups and downs of daily life and the moment soon passes. If, however, your self-esteem is low, this perception of being rubbish can permeate the whole of your life.

In general, people with a healthy self-esteem accept who they are and what they are, realising that not being good at everything does not devalue them at all. Those with low self-esteem tend to rely on present performance to 'grade' themselves and need the approbation of others in order to feel valued. Even then, the feelings of satisfaction that come from doing something well may be short-lived. Of course, extremely high self-esteem isn't always healthy and can border on narcissism, and at the same time, there is nothing wrong with humility.

Self-esteem is one area of our lives where our childhood experiences can't help but shape our adult persona. A childhood that was full of praise, love, hugs and respect is more likely to contribute to a healthy sense of self-esteem than a childhood devoid of these things. For us, as adults, it is too late and our die has been cast; knowing the causes and effects though can help us to bring up healthy children.

As a child, I was always expected to be perfect and can clearly remember, on getting 99 per cent for an English exam, being asked where the other 1 per cent was. The person who inflicted that on me did so in the belief that it would cause me to try harder and, in a way, it did. Unfortunately, the upshot is that I am never satisfied with anything less than perfect, even though, as an adult, I know that this is impossible to achieve in everything I do. If I am less than perfect in anything, I feel that I have failed, not only in that particular project but in life in general.

That is one manifestation of low self-esteem, but there are others. For instance, lack of self-worth can cause problems with forming and maintaining relationships, because the sufferer always feels not quite good enough or unable to live up to the standards of a previous partner. It can lead to underachievement due to a feeling of 'Why bother, I'll never make the grade anyway'.

I have described here the effects of which I have personal knowledge, though of course there are others of varying severity. At its most destructive, low self-esteem can lead to a vicious spiral of negative thinking, which drags the sufferer lower and lower into a trough of not believing in oneself. The consequence of this can even lead to suicide.

As it is our inner voice that tells us the lies about what failures we are, the Rational Emotive Behaviour Therapy exercise (see page 19) can be good to do here, providing that one has the insight to realise what the activating event is and to understand that it is negative self-talk that is causing the problem. Sometimes, one can feel so negative that rather than rebuke that inner voice, the person agrees with it. In this instance, I suggest that you leave the REBT exercises until later and attempt some free journaling based on the following concepts first.

Journaling towards healthy self-esteem

If you are serious about self-improvement then, after the exercises in the previous chapter on learning who you are, these are probably the most important exercises you will ever undertake.

I have something to offer

The purpose of journaling based on the following prompts is for you to get a handle on exactly where your self-esteem is weak – sometimes it is weak only in certain areas. You should aim to write for 15 to 20 minutes on each prompt, undertaking only one in any individual journaling session.

❀ If you make mistakes, will others reject you? Why?

❀ What do people at work think of you? Why?

❀ What do your friends and family think of you? Why?

❀ What do you think of you? Why?

❀ For what reasons should people love you?

❀ What have you got to say that others will find interesting?

❀ If you take off your mask and act as your true self, will others still like you? Why? Why not?

❀ Do you think that others make friends more easily than you? Why? Why not?

❀ Does your sense of success or failure rely on the perception of others? Why? Why not?

❀ If you left work next week without telling anybody, would your absence be noticed? Why? Why not?

❀ If you have an idea or a suggestion that nobody else agrees with, how does it make you feel? Why?

Dear me

Write a letter to your five-year-old self, using the present tense. Tell her how loved and valued she is and how precious she is to your parents/grandparents/whoever you knew loved you at that time. It might help if you have a photograph of yourself at that age in front of you, but it is not essential.

Self-nurturing

This group of journaling prompts is about learning to value yourself, because once you do that you will be more inclined to believe that others value you too.

❀ Write about your successes and your strengths. It may help to start a file of certificates, awards and thank you cards. If you choose to keep a rewards file, keep it where you can easily see it and access it when you are feeling down.

❀ Write yourself a list of simple, cheap rewards then, when you have a success, a triumph or when you help somebody to feel better about themselves, have one of the rewards on your list. As you tick off the rewards, you will begin to realise that you are a valuable friend, colleague and member of your community.

❀ For a period of a week or so, try to be aware of every time you make a self-deprecating comment and make a note of what it was you said. At the end of the week analyse these comments to see if there is any trend or pattern, which can tell you when it is you feel most ill at ease. You can then go on to dispute these self-deprecatory remarks in your journal. Imagine that it wasn't you who made the remarks but somebody else. What would you say in your defence? This is a freeform version of the REBT exercise and, if you find it easier, you may wish to use the template in the Resources section (see page 168).

28 *Self-image*

Self-image is about how we see ourselves and how we imagine we are seen by others. It is one of a whole group of constructs that psychologists use to describe elements of the self. In the previous chapter we looked at self-esteem, a slightly different concept in that it refers to our general feelings of self-worth or the value we place upon ourselves.

In this set of exercises we are not looking at how worthy we think we are, but rather the picture we hold of ourselves in our minds. This picture will be based on a number of things, including our beliefs about who and what we are, and our abilities. It could be argued that self-image is the basis on which we build all the other constructs of self. However, our self-image can be faulty because it can remain set in the past or be based on false beliefs. If you think about who you were, say, ten years ago and compare that person with who you are now, it is likely that life events have caused you to grow spiritually and to develop new skills and personality traits. Sometimes, though, our self-image doesn't keep up with this development and our image of ourselves becomes stuck in the past.

The self-image of many women is focused on the physical self, and this image is often distorted. In her 1993 book *Pleasure: The Truth about Female Sexuality*, Margaret Leroy writes about a survey carried out by a women's glossy magazine. In the survey, 75 per cent of women aged 18–35 described themselves as fat. The data that they gave for weight and height, however, implied that only 25 per cent of them were actually overweight, suggesting that 50 per cent of them had a faulty self-image. The same survey also found that nearly half of these women would choose to lose ten pounds in preference to meeting their soul mate or achieving their career ambition.

Journaling towards an improved self-image

Some of the work that follows asks you to look at your self-image using the REBT framework, whilst other writing tasks are designed to help you assess what aspects of your looks can be improved and whether or not you want to do the work that is required to make a change.

What do I see?

Start by doing some timed writings of ten to 20 minutes using the following prompts:

❀ When I look in the mirror I see …

❀ When I look in the mirror I would like to see …

❀ Things I like about the way I look.

❀ Things I don't like about the way I look.

If the things you don't like are within your power to change with a healthy diet and exercise, and if you would feel better about yourself if you made these changes, then your next journaling exercise should be to compile the following lists:

❀ What I would like to change about the way I look.

❀ What is within my power to change about the way I look.

❀ What is not within my power to change about the way I look.

Targets and self-acceptance

If you feel healthy, and your doctor has no concerns about your physical health, there is no need to change anything, although a healthier diet could do us all a bit of good. With that in mind, I offer you the following timed writing exercises:

❀ How I could I make my diet healthier.

❀ How I could incorporate exercise into my daily life.

❋ How I could dress to look my best.

❋ What I need to add to my wardrobe.

❋ What I need to lose from my wardrobe.

❋ Why I do/do not wish to eat a healthier diet/get more exercise.

❋ Why I get upset about the way I look.

❋ How I could play up my best features to deflect from my not so good features.

❋ My destructive self-talk concerning my looks is ... (use the REBT form here, see page 168).

❋ My plan of action to become happier about the way I look is ...

To maximise your chances of reaching whatever target you set yourself, conventional wisdom recommends you set a date for achievement. For me, however, this can be a double-edged sword; on the one hand it gives me something to strive towards but, on the other hand, as I near the date I have set with little possibility of reaching my target, my self-esteem takes a pummelling.

Nothing worth having comes without hard work and application, and that applies to both self-acceptance and doing something to bring you a more positive self-image. My task is to choose which course of hard work I wish to undertake – that which would lead to a body that I would view as more attractive or that which would lead to me accepting my body as it is. This insight has come to me whilst writing this chapter, which is proof, I think, that writing things down helps to clarify the thought processes and bring about a deeper understanding of personal issues.

Saying goodbye to destructive habits

If your self-image is unhealthy, you are going to need to make some radical changes in your patterns of thinking. If you have gone so far down the poor self-image road that you have an eating disorder or suffer from a condition where your self-image is preventing you from living a normal life I urge to you seek medical advice. However, even whilst receiving traditional medical support and treatment, journaling will help you to let go of your self-destructive habits.

At the beginning of this process, you may find that you have more questions than answers. Try timed writing for the usual ten to 20 minutes using the following questions:

❋ If I let go of my need to be perfect, how will I feel?

❋ If I don't obsess about my self-image, what will my thoughts turn to?

❋ If I don't have an eating disorder, what else will make me special?

Giving up a habitual way of being, no matter how destructive it has been, will not be easy; the chances are that you will miss that way of being. As my mother used to say 'You'd miss a gammy arm if they cut it off'.

Try writing the following letters:

❋ Write a letter saying goodbye to those destructive habits. It needn't be a harsh letter, after all, these habits have served you well for some period of time and you might want to thank them for that. However, tell these habits that they are no longer needed in your life.

❋ Now write a welcoming letter to the new habits you are ready to embrace. Explain to these new habits how you hope they will help you both in healing the past and moving forward to a healthier self-image.

❋ Finally, write how it feels to be free of your self-destructive nature. Describe the strength you feel, having made the decision to move forwards to a healthier and happier future.

29 Work and Career Motivation

This is the chapter for you if you are feeling bored or under-utilised at work, or if your motivation is non-existent. There can be many reasons for this lack of enthusiasm, ranging from mid-life crisis, office politics or just realising that you are in the wrong job.

Bearing in mind that if you have a full-time job it will occupy most of your waking hours, it makes sense to ensure that your work works for you. It's nice to earn a lot of money but I think that many of us who have been miserable at work eventually come to the conclusion that what is in your pay packet at the end of the month isn't the be all and end all.

If you've been in a job for many years, you probably feel safe there. Moving out of one's comfort zone is never easy and, for some people, it is very traumatic. Change is always difficult but sometimes it is essential to change so that you can move forward.

Journaling to ensure work is working for you

The following exercises should help you to discover how you really feel about your current job and what you would like to be doing instead. They should also help motivate you to make the necessary changes.

I must have

This exercise involves making a list of the important things in your life, things that you would not want to live without. Whilst I am not looking to leave my current job in the short term, I am well aware that I am coming up to the normal age of retirement for midwives, and that I have no desire to give up work completely. This means that I need to plan ahead. The following are some examples from my own list:

* A permanent and comfortable home.

* Warmth.

* Healthy food.

* Time with my husband and family.

* Regular and quality sleep.

* Less stress.

Using my own example, my job provides me with the permanent comfortable home, decent food on my table and the wherewithal to pay my heating bills. However, it actively causes me intense stress, takes away quality time with my husband and, because shift work is involved, affects my sleep pattern and the quality of my sleep. In fact, the only thing going for it in terms of must haves is that it pays the bills. My consolation is that I know that in a few years' time I will be able to put the lessons I've learned from these exercises into practice.

I would like

Having decided your must haves, your next task is to think seriously about what you would like. Once again, I have used my own list as an example:

* To work from home.

* To use my writing talent.

* To help others, particularly women, to understand themselves.

* To give women the strength to be empowered.

* To utilise the skills and knowledge I have gained in my own life.

I can offer

Employment is, of course, a two-way thing. Your employer, or society, gains from whatever it is you have to give. Think hard about what you can offer, taking into account life skills as well as taught skills. There is far more emphasis in today's job and educational markets on previous experiential learning; people realise that what you have learned just by being alive and functioning in society is of great importance. My own example reads:

* Strength of character.

* Innate writing ability.

* Empathy.

* Personal experience of childbirth, motherhood and menopause.

* Proven ability to survive difficult circumstances.

* A deep understanding of women's issues.

* A commitment to improving women's lives.

* An ability to empower and enthuse.

* Intelligence.

* Research skills.

* Office and administration skills.

* An enquiring mind.

If you look at my list, you will note that I haven't mentioned any of my jobs at all, I have simply listed the knowledge, experience or strengths I have gained from undertaking them. If you have stayed at home as a mother and never done a day's paid work in your life, you can still make a list like mine because you have become adept at multi-tasking, teaching, nurturing, cooking, budgeting, liaising and many other tasks too numerous to mention.

Carrying out these journaling exercises should have piqued your interest about what is on offer to you in the world of work that would utilise your skills and inclinations to the full, whilst at the same time providing the things you need and want in your life. There will, as in all areas of life, be limitations. My list above suggests to me that life coaching would be an ideal goal for me to pursue, but courses are expensive and out of my financial reach at present. What is within my reach, though, is trying to sell my writing as articles or books.

My favourite things

This time list the five things you enjoy doing most – things like walking, cooking, writing, going to the gym – whatever it is you would rather be doing than being at work.

What I want to achieve

Make a list of things you would like to achieve in your life, and be honest with yourself. At the risk of embarrassment, these are mine:

* Fame.

* Money.

* To make a positive difference.

* To be remembered for making a positive difference.

My options

Having undertaken the analysis of where you are and what you have to offer, the next logical step is to identify the options open to you. This is not just a matter of looking in the paper for jobs, but rather of actively marketing yourself. Try the following:

* Write about your previous successes.

* Do a SWOT analysis, either using the template in the Resources section (see page 181) or simply free-writing under the appropriate headings (strengths, weaknesses, opportunities, threats) in your journal.

* List all possible ways of finding the job you want. For instance, there will be advertisements in the local job

pages, you could write to the companies that may be able to offer the sort of job you are looking for, you could join clubs or online groups and network.

❀ Start to put together a CV that is based on your previous achievements as identified above.

❀ Write a timed plan for how you will move forward.

The rest, of course, is up to you. The internet and the bookshops are filled with the information you need to help you narrow down your choices even further. However, I suspect that, deep in your heart, you know exactly what it is you want to do. If that is the case and you have the necessary abilities and life-experience, my suggestion is that you just go for it. The exercises in this chapter should have given you the self-belief to do just that.

30 Goal, Reality, Options, Will

I would like to finish the exercise section of this book with something that is short and sweet and that I have filched from the world of personal coaching. GROW, standing for Goal, Reality, Options and Will, is an exercise designed to get you thinking realistically about the options open to you. It is applicable to any area of your life where you would like to progress. In terms of personal growth, I suspect it would encompass all of the things covered in this section and more – it is a powerful trick to keep up your sleeve. The instructions are very simple.

❦ **G**   Write about your **goal** in your journal. Be very specific and write exactly what it is you want to achieve.

❦ **R**   Write about the **reality** of achieving your goals from your current situation. In other words, from where you are now, is your goal realistic or will you have to put things into place to make it more achievable?

❦ **O**   What **options** are open to you to help you make sure that your goal is realistic and achievable? Do you need training? Do you need time? Analyse all the things that stand in your way and list your options for dealing with these things.

❦ **W**   What **will** you do? This is about making a plan of action that will lead towards achievement of your goal. For example, if your goal is to make money from your tarot reading skills your 'wills' could be:

*   I will place an advertorial in the local newspaper explaining about the use of tarot for personal growth.

* I will book space in the local community centre/new age shop every other Saturday afternoon and sell tarot readings.

* I will put together a training programme and advertise lessons in the local free paper.

Afterword

I hope that you have found the exercises within this book useful and thought provoking. As I have already said, I believe them to be groundbreaking because they are based on specific psychological tools and methods: tools and methods that are known to be effective in changing negative thought processes into positive ones. My anticipation, though, is that you will use my suggestions as a basis for creating your own writing exercises, tailoring them for the situation in which you find yourself.

The other thing I would like you to understand is that there are many alternatives to 'straight' writing prompts. One of the triggers that I find most powerful is the tarot; the exercises that you can base on this beautiful oracular system are worthy of a book in itself. The cards particularly lend themselves to a meditative style of journaling, which is useful at transformative stages of your life. Other things you could think about using as prompts are numerology, art, photographs, dreams and family history. In the Resources section you will find a list of journaling prompts which, if you are a 'word' person like me, will be an excellent starting point (see page 182).

Remember that you needn't restrict yourself to writing. You can use all sorts of creative media to make a journal truly yours. It very much depends on how your mind works. I think in words but I am well aware that some people think in colours and others think in terms of smell and touch. Why not add colour to your journal – you could start off simply by using different coloured pens and, as you become more confident and at ease with recording your innermost thoughts, you could move on to other media such as paints, collage and applied fabrics. The secret is that it really doesn't matter, because you are writing to and for yourself. Your journal is a place to be truly yourself, to fly your colours and fight your fight with no holds barred. The benefits of journaling are here for you to grasp; you will be amazed that such a seemingly simple tool can bring such remarkable results – and the rewards will last you a lifetime.

Pick up your pen and write.

Resources

In this section of the book you will find templates for frequently used processes, along with a number of other tools that you might find useful in journaling.

The ABC of negative thinking is a REBT tool that comes from Dr Ellis's work on thinking realistically rather than thinking positively. You will find full references to his work in the Bibliography (see page 186).

I am indebted to my husband, Keith Sandland, who, as a quality manager and consultant in the information technology sector, uses some of these tools on a daily basis in his work. We have both felt for some time that these tools are equally applicable to 'personal management'. Think of yourself as a quality management project!

I also need to thank Phil Croft, a colleague and friend of mine from TABI (The Tarot Association for the British Isles). In his 'real' life, Phil is a director of Impromptu Ltd, a corporate role-play supplier. His job involves preparing and facilitating role-play exercises for teams of people in the working environment, including the NHS. He was a mine of useful information, introducing me to some of the life coaching tools.

Thank you both.

These resources are included on the following pages:

The ABC of negative thinking	168
Relaxation and meditation	170
Grief theories	174
Cost/benefit analysis	175
SMART objectives	176
Clustering	177
Social readjustment rating scale	178
Medication chart	180
SWOT analysis	181
Journaling prompts	182

The ABC of negative thinking

A Activating event

(blank box)

❊ What is it that has upset me? What event has caused me to feel awful?

❊ What has happened to make me feel as I do?

B Irrational beliefs

(blank box)

❊ What do I believe that makes this situation so awful for me? What are my 'musts'?

C Consequences

(blank box)

❊ How do these irrational beliefs make me feel or act? Am I angry, scared, jealous, hurt, guilty, sad?

D Dispute

Is what I'm feeling logical? What benefits am I gaining from feeling this way? Can I prove that my beliefs are correct?

E Effective new belief and positive emotional consequence

Having understood that my beliefs surrounding this event are unrealistic, what is a more logical way to feel about the event and how does that new way of understanding cause me to feel emotionally?

Relaxation and meditation

I do not propose to present you with a fully guided meditation. There are many books and CDs on the market that deal exclusively with this area. What I offer you is a modification of the relaxation technique that served me well over many years of facilitating antenatal classes. It will lead you to a state of deep relaxation in which you will be more able to access the intuitive right-hand side of your brain.

Initially, you will probably have to keep looking at the prompts or you could try recording your voice to play back later, remembering to leave the necessary spaces for actions. However, this is a simple exercise so you will eventually be able to do it with no outside help at all.

Wearing loose non-restrictive clothing, and ensuring that you will not be disturbed for half an hour or so, sit in a comfortable, straight-backed chair, with both your feet firmly on the floor. Work slowly through the following process. Probably the most important thing to remember is that there is no rush, rather you are aiming for the reverse: a slow and sure reduction of your breathing rate and brain activity, which will leave you relaxed and open to your subconscious.

* As you sit in your chair, close your eyes and listen to your breathing. Concentrate on the air as you slowly breathe it in through your nose and gently breathe it out through your mouth. Once you have established a rhythmic, slow pattern of breathing continue concentrating on the pattern until you feel totally relaxed.

* When you are suitably relaxed, imagine that there are roots growing from your feet. As you think about them, you can feel them going down through each floor below you until they reach the cool, damp earth. Then imagine the roots gently piercing the surface of the soil and growing ever further down into the earth itself. You can feel these roots anchoring you safely to the earth and, at the same time, drawing sustenance from the earth and transporting it slowly but surely up into your body as you sit in your chair.

✾ As you sit there, safely anchored in time and space, feel the sustenance and energy of the earth as it enters through the soles of your feet and travels up to your heart. Imagine this energy as a bright, softly glowing white light. Feel your heart pump this life-giving source around your body, energising all of your cells and bringing new life to them whilst, at the same time, relaxing you and making you feel at one with the universe.

✾ As the life source reaches the base of your spine, imagine that there is a closed rose in that place. As it fills with the life source, imagine the rose opening and glowing with a soft white light. Eventually, the rose begins to spin.

✾ Next, imagine the life source travelling from the base of your spine to a place in the pit of your stomach. Again imagine the rose that is there opening, petal by petal and beginning to glow with that same gentle light. Eventually, as the flower begins to spin, feel the energy source travel up to the centre of your chest, your solar plexus.

✾ Once again, imagine that the rose slowly opens and begins to glow. Once it is freely spinning, feel the life source move to the base of your throat where the same phenomenon happens – the rose opens slowly, glows white and begins spinning.

✾ Do the same as the life force reaches the middle of your forehead, your third-eye. The rose opens, glows and spins before the life force travels to the top of your head and the final rose in your body opens very slowly, petal by petal. The light that glows is gentle yet powerful and feels as if it must come from the Divine. Set the rose spinning.

✾ Once the rose at your crown is freely spinning, you feel the energy of the earth as a bright, white light as it emerges and travels a little way above you.

❀ When the light is a short distance above your head, imagine that it divides into two and travels back down to the earth. As it travels, it leaves behind it a shining white bubble of protection.

❀ As you sit quietly and calmly within this bubble, with your feet anchored to the floor, know that you are safe and that nothing can harm you.

❀ In the protection of your bubble, allow random images to cross your mind, perhaps playing on the screen that is situated at the site of your third eye in your forehead – your mind's eye. You do not need to concentrate, just let an image slide across your mind and fade away as it is followed by another and then another.

❀ When you have seen all that you need to see, it is time to return to the real world. This is simply a matter of reversing the above procedure. So, you will draw the white-light bubble back up to the crown of your head and through your body, retracing its steps. As it passes through each flower, feel the light recede and the spinning slow and stop. Then see the petals close one by one. Only once a flower is back in its original closed state, will you move the light back to the next flower.

❀ When all the flowers are tightly closed, feel the energy source exit through the soles of your feet and travel back down your anchoring roots into the earth, where it came from.

❀ Slowly, retract your roots, knowing that you can plant them again whenever you have the need to feel strong and supported by the earth.

❀ Once more, concentrate on your breathing and begin to hear and feel the everyday world around you.

❀ Slowly open your eyes and return to your life.

❀ Commit to memory the insights you gained in your relaxed state before you leave your chair.

❀ It is probable that you will feel quite spaced out following this exercise so you should have something to eat or drink to make you feel more grounded. A glass of water will suffice if you don't want to eat.

❀ Write about your insights in your journal, letting your pen take you wherever it wants to go.

❀ This is a powerful exercise that continues to grow in power the more experienced you become at 'going into yourself'.

Grief theories

The grid below illustrates how grief theories have changed since the first description of the grief process back in 1944. The process described by Kübler-Ross in 1969 is still the best known. The five phases listed here are expanded upon in her book *Death and Dying*. Because it recognises the anger of grief, this is the theory that resonates most with me. You may find that one of the other descriptions mirrors your own experience more closely.

Lindemann 1944	Kübler-Ross 1969	Parkes 1975	Bowlby 1981	Worden 1991
Shock	Denial	Numbness	Numbing	Acceptance of the loss
Acute mourning	Anger	Searching/ pining	Searching	Working through pain and grief
Resolution	Guilt	Depression	Disorganisation and despair	Adjusting to life without the deceased
	Depression	Recovery	Adjustment in new life	Reinvestment
	Acceptance			

Cost/benefit analysis

To decide between . . . . and . . . .

Date . . . .

Option A	
Advantages (Benefits)	Disadvantages (Costs)

Option B	
Advantages (Benefits)	Disadvantages (Costs)

SMART objectives

Specify what you want to achieve.

How will you **measure** your progress?

Can you **achieve** your objective? Think about things that would definitely stop you achieving your objective, like lack of expertise or physical impossibility.

At this time in your life, do you have the resources to make the achievement of your objective **realistic**?

Come up with a sensible **time** frame and set yourself a deadline.

Clustering

Your clustering exercise need not be as tidy as this one! For instance, if Thought 1 elicits seven more thoughts, draw lines from Thought 1's circle to seven more circles, and write down these thoughts. Messy but powerful.

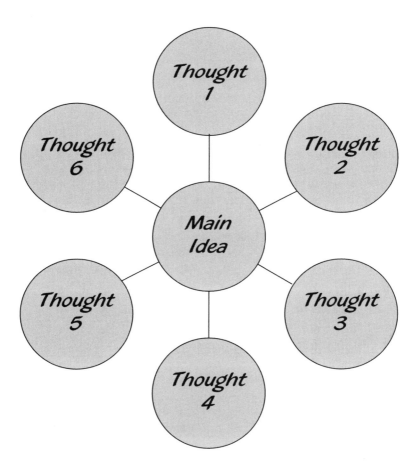

Social readjustment rating scale

(Holmes-Rahe, 1967)

Go through the scale below and add up your score for the past 12 months. Analyse the results as follows:

* ✿ **150 points or less:** Relatively low amount of life changes this year and, therefore, susceptibility to change-induced stress is low.

* ✿ **150 to 300 points:** 50 per cent chance of a health breakdown in the next two years.

* ✿ **300 points or more:** Odds of health breakdown in the next two years increased to 80 per cent.

If you are aware that your life is in a difficult phase, it is possible to take steps to try to minimise the negative impact. Do keep in mind, though, that these are all events that are part of a normal life and are things that most people have to deal with at some time or another. It is only when a number of them coincide that you may feel you have a problem.

Event	Impact
Death of spouse	100
Divorce	73
Separation	65
Jail term	63
Death of close family member	63
Personal illness or injury	53
Marriage	50
Lost job	47
Marital reconciliation	45
Retirement	45
Change in health of family member	44
Pregnancy	40
Sex difficulties	39

Gain of new family member	39
Business readjustment	38
Change in financial state	38
Death of close friend	37
Change to a different line of work	36
Change in number of arguments with spouse	35
A large mortgage or loan	30
Foreclosure of mortgage or loan	30
Change in responsibilities at work	29
Son or daughter leaving home	29
Trouble with in-laws	29
Outstanding personal achievement	28
Spouse begins or stops work	26
Begin or end of school or college	26
Change in living conditions	25
Change in personal habits	24
Trouble with boss	23
Change in work hours or conditions	20
Change in residence	20
Change in school or college	20
Change in recreation	19
Change in church activities	19
Change in social activities	18
A moderate loan or mortgage	17
Change in sleeping habits	16
Change in number of family get-togethers	15
Change in eating habits	15
Holiday	13
Christmas	12
Minor violations of law	11

Medication chart

Medication	Dose	Route of administration	Frequency	Comments

Double check whether the dosage is microgram or milligram. Ensure it is entered correctly.

Medical abbreviations

po = take by mouth
pr = insert into rectum
od = once a day
tds = three times a day
nocté = take at night

pv = insert into vagina
sl = place under tongue
bd = twice a day
qds = four times a day
mane = take in the morning

SWOT analysis

This is a simple tool for ascertaining your current situation.

Strengths	Weaknesses

Opportunities	Threats

Journaling prompts

- The first day of winter
- Midsummer
- Christmas
- Fun
- My best friend
- Trees
- The sky
- A thunder storm
- Mother
- Father
- Son
- Daughter
- My birthday
- Fear
- If I had unlimited money
- If I had unlimited time
- When I'm angry
- When I'm sad
- The last time I cried
- Honesty
- Lies
- Betrayal
- War
- If I were famous
- Shoes
- Clothes
- The edge
- Boundaries
- Perfume
- Outside my window
- Behind that door
- Shame
- Goals
- Achievements
- Failure
- If I could do it all again
- Dreaming
- Right now
- What's missing?

- Principles
- When I die
- Love
- Insanity
- Depression
- Poverty
- Darkness
- Sunshine
- When my eyes are closed
- Roses
- Emptiness
- Life after death
- God
- Spirituality
- Ghosts
- Clairvoyance
- The one thing I'd save
- Forgiveness
- Belief
- Admiration
- Solitude
- Rain
- What if
- If the world ended
- Absence
- Pain
- Laughter
- Joy
- The human soul
- Humility
- Secrets
- Shadows
- Others see me as
- I think I am
- Relationships
- Shopping
- Eating
- Reading
- Age

Useful Information

Writing equipment

Arthritis Research Campaign
Copeman House
St Mary's Court
St Mary's Gate
Chesterfield
Derbyshire S41 7TD
Telephone: 0870 850 5000
Suppliers of big pens with finger grips that are easier to use if you suffer from arthritis

Oberon Design
1813 Empire Industrial Ct
Santa Rosa
California
95403
USA
www.oberondesign.com
I have three of this company's hand-tooled leather journals; they are expensive but exquisite

Stone Marketing Limited
10 Sovereign Way
Tonbridge
Kent TN9 1RH
Telephone: 01732 771771
Suppliers of Paperblank diaries and journals

Journaling prompts

Cilla Conway, visionary artist
www.cillaconway.com
Cilla's 'Devas of Creation' cards are a superb tool for stimulating the intuitive brain and jump starting your journaling when you are at a loss for words. Her Intuitive Tarot is a more traditional tarot deck and is also ideal for giving you a kick-start.

TABI
www.tabi.org.uk
If you have more than a passing interest in tarot, then have a look at the website of The Tarot Association of the British Isles, an organisation whose mission is to help ensure that tarot readers are regulated and undertake to abide by sound ethics.

Helplines

Association for Postnatal Illness
Telephone: 020 7386 0868
www.apni.org

British Association of Art Therapists
Telephone: 020 7686 4216
www.baat.org

British Association for Behavioural and Cognitive Psychotherapies (BABCP)
Telephone: 01254 875277
www.babcp.com

The Child Death Helpline
Helpline: 0800 282986
Open every evening 7–10pm;
Monday to Friday 10am–1pm
and Wednesday 1–4pm

Cruse Bereavement Care
Telephone: 0870 167 1677
www.cruselochaber.freeuk.com

Department of Health Publications
www.doh.gov.uk
Search for 'mental health publication' and then click on the link to 'Mental health publications'. Many of the publications listed are downloadable; 'Choosing talking therapies' is particularly relevant to this book.

Depression Alliance
www.depressionalliance.org
Click on the 'contact us' link and then on the 'groups' link to be taken to a list of local groups and their contact details.

Eating Disorders Association
Adult helpline: 0845 634 1414
Youthline (up to and including 18 years of age): 0845 6347650
www.edauk.com

The Foundation for the Study of Infant Deaths
Artillery House
11–19 Artillery Row
London SW1P 1RT
Helpline: 020 7233 2090
www.sids.org.uk

Manic Depression Fellowship (MDF)
Telephone (UK): 08456 340450
Telephone (rest of the world):
0044 207 793 2600
www.mdf.org.uk

The Mental Health Foundation
9th Floor
Sea Containers House
20 Upper Ground
London SE1 9QB
Telephone: 020 7803 1100
www.mentalhealth.org.uk

Mind (National Association for Mental Health)
PO Box 277
Manchester M60 3XN
Telephone: 08457 660 163
(Open Monday to Friday, 9.15am –5.15pm)
www.mind.org.uk

The National Association for People Abused in Childhood
NAPAC
42 Curtain Road
London EC2A 3NH
www.napac.org.uk

National Self-harm Network
PO Box 16190
London NW1 3WW
www.nsn.co.uk
email:
nshn@dividedwefall.fsnet.co.uk

NHS Direct
Telephone: 0845 46 47
www.nhsdirect.nhs.uk

Parentline Plus
Telephone: 0808 800 2222
www.parentlineplus.org.uk
Offers support and help to parents

Relate (previously Marriage Guidance Association)
Telephone: 0845 456 1310
www.relate.org.uk

Samaritans
Telephone: 08457 90 90 90
In your local telephone directory under 'S'
www.samaritans.org

Survivors of Incest Anonymous
www.siawso.org

Bibliography

Introduction to Journaling

Allen, Pat B, *Art is a Way of Knowing: a guide to self-knowledge and spiritual fulfilment through creativity*, Shambhala Publications, USA, 1995

Aristotle (transl J I Beare), 'On Memory and Reminiscence', 350 BCE, The Internet Classics Archive: http://classics.mit.edu, accessed 28 November 2005

Barber, Vicky, *Explore Yourself Through Art: a practical guide for using a wide range of art forms for self-expression, personal growth and problem-solving*, Carrol and Brown Publishers Limited, 2002

McNiff, Shaun, *Art as Medicine: Creating a therapy of the imagination*, Shambhala Publications, USA, 1992

Therapeutic Writing

Adams, Kathleen, *Journal to the Self*, Warner Books, USA, 1990

Boehnert, Diana, 'Journaling for Health', *Complements Integrative Medicine Quarterly News* 1:2, September 2004

Pennebaker, James W, 'Telling Stories: The Health Benefits of Narrative', *Literature and Medicine* 19:1, Spring 2000, pp 3–18

Pennebaker, James W, *Opening Up: The Healing Power of Expressing Emotions*, Guildford Press, USA, 1997

Talking Therapies

Beck, Aaron T, *Cognitive Therapy and the Emotional Disorders*, Penguin Books, 1979

Burns, David B, *Feeling Good: The New Mood Therapy*, Avon Books, 1999

Clark, D A and Beck, A T, *Scientific foundations of cognitive theory and therapy of depression*, John Wiley and Sons, USA, 1999

Cooney, Geraldine, 'Choosing Talking Therapies?', *Patient Information Leaflet*, Department of Health, UK

Ellis, Albert, *A Guide to Rational Living*, Wilshire Book Company, USA, 1975

Ellis, Albert, *How to Live with a Neurotic*, Wilshire Book Company, USA, 1979

Ellis, Albert, *Overcoming Destructive Beliefs, Feelings, and Behaviours: New Directions for Rational Emotive Behaviour Therapy*, Prometheus Books, USA, 2001

Ellis, Albert, *The Road to Tolerance: The Philosophy of Rational Emotive Behaviour Therapy*, Prometheus Books, USA, 2004

Faulkner, Alison and de Ponte, Paul, 'Talking Therapies', *Update*, The Mental Health Foundation, 2000

A Brief History of Journaling

Blood, Rebecca, *The Weblog Handbook: Practical advice on creating and maintaining your blog*, Perseus Book Group, USA, 2002

Book of Blogs Inc, *I Blog, Therefore I Am*, Authorhouse, USA, 2005

Knights, Dr Mark, 'Diaries of the Seventeenth Century', *BBC History*, www.bbc.co.uk/history, accessed November 2005

Lifshin, Lyn (ed), *Ariadne's Thread: A collection of contemporary women's journals*, HarperCollins, USA, 1982

Lyons, Paul K, 'The Diary Junction', www.pikle.demon.co.uk/diaryjunction, accessed November 2005

Mallon, Thomas, *A Book of One's Own: People and their diaries*, Ruminator Books (reprint), USA, 1995

Skills and Equipment
Travis, F, 'The TM technique and creativity: A longitudinal study of Cornell University undergraduates', *Journal of Creative Behaviour 13*, pp 169–180, 1979

Wikipedia Contributors, 'Mind-Body Intervention', *Wikipedia*, The Free Encyclopaedia, accessed 11 August 2006

Poetry for the Terrified
Fry, Stephen, *The Ode Less Travelled: Unlocking the poet within*, Hutchinson, London, 2005

What is Healing?
Danner, Snowdon and Friesen, 'Positive emotions in early life and longevity: Findings from the nun study', *Journal of Personality and Social Psychology*, 80, pp 804, 2001

Gallo, Linda and Matthews, Karen, 'Understanding the Association Between Socioeconomic Status and Physical Health: Do Negative Emotions Play a Role?', *Psychological Bulletin 129*:1 pp 10–51, American Psychological Association Inc, 2003

Mate, Gabor, *When the Body Says No: The Cost of Hidden Stress*, Vintage, Canada, 2004

Bereavement
'About Grief and Bereavement', www.elisabethkublerross.com, accessed 29 May 2006

Read, Sue, 'Loss and bereavement: a nursing response' within 'Continuing Professional Development: Patient support', *Nursing Standard* 16:37, pp 47–53, May 2002

The Death of a Child
Rate of Sudden Infant Deaths per 1,000 live births 1989–2004 England and Wales, National Statistics website: www.statistics.gov.uk, Crown copyright material is reproduced with the permission of the Controller of HMSO

Marriage, Relationships and Divorce
Gray, J, *What Your Mother Didn't Tell You and Your Father Didn't Know: Advanced relationship skills for better communication and lasting intimacy*, Harper Collins, USA, 1994

Rich, P and Copans, S, *The Healing Journal for Couples: Your Journal of Mutual Discovery*, John Wiley, USA, 1998

Emotional Health and Healing
Brostoff, Professor Jonathan and Gamlin, Linda, *The Complete Guide to Food Allergy and Intolerance*, Bloomsbury, 1989

DesMaisons, Kathleen, *Potatoes not Prozac*, Simon and Schuster, USA, 1998

Geary, Amanda, 'Food and Mood: a complementary treatment for mental health issues', *Positive Health: Complementary Medicine for the 21st Century*, Positive Health Publications Ltd, March 2000

Geary, Amanda, *The Food and Mood Self-help Survey Report*, London, 2002

187

Depression

Jamison, Kay Redfield, *Touched with Fire: Manic-depressive illness and the artistic temperament*, Simon and Schuster Ltd, USA, 1996

Woolston, Chris, *Consumer Health Interactive, My Health Website*, www.myhealthwellmark.com, accessed 1 July 2006

Natasha W, *Illness Journaling*, personal website, http://pages.zdnet.com/tatty/mymentaltrampoline, accessed 8 July 2006

Addictions

Ellis, Albert, *When AA Doesn't Work For You: Rational steps to quitting alcohol*, Barricade Books, USA, 1992

Ellis, Albert and Tate, Philip, *Alcohol: How to give it up and be glad you did*, Sharp Press, 1996

Ewing, John A, 'Detecting Alcoholism: The CAGE Questionnaire', *Journal of the American Medical Association 252:14*, pp 1905–1907, 1984

Recovering from Childhood Abuse

Harris, Thomas A, *I'm OK – You're OK*, Harper and Row, USA, 1969

James, William, 'The Stream of Consciousness', *Psychology*, Chapter XI, New York, 1892, The Internet Classics Archive: http://classics.mit.edu, accessed 28 November 2005

Eating Disorders

'Eating disorders: anorexia nervosa, bulimia nervosa and related eating disorders', *Understanding NICE guidance: a guide for people with eating disorders, their advocates and carers, and the public*, National Institute for Clinical Excellence, London, 2004

Stress

Friedman, Meyer and Rosenman, Ray, 'Association of specific overt behaviour pattern with blood and cardiovascular findings', *Journal of the American Medical Association*, 1959

Holmes, T and Rahe, R, 'Holmes-Rahe Readjustment Scale', *Journal of Psychosomatic Research II*, 1967

'Autism and Stress', Ivanhoe citing Heather Kohn in *'Medical Breakthroughs'*, www.ivanhoe.com/channels, accessed 23 April 2006

Anger Management

'Modeling (NLP)', Wikipedia Contributors, *Wikipedia*, The Free Encyclopaedia, accessed 11 August 2006

Physical Health

Astin, John, et al, 'Mind-Body Medicine: State of the Science, Implications for Practice', *Journal of the American Board of Family Medicine 16*, pp 131–147, 2003

Beck, Eunice, 'Writing as Therapy: Why Chronic Fatigue Syndrome and Fibromyalgia Patients Can Benefit from Journaling', *Chronic Fatigue.com*, www.chronicfatiguesupport.com, accessed 27 November 2005

Campo, Rafael, '"The Medical Humanities", for Lack of a Better Term', JAMA – *Journal of the American Medical Association*, 294 pp 1009–1011, 2005

Carroll, Robert, 'Finding the Words to Say It: The Healing Power of Poetry', *eCAM 2*, pp 161–172, 2005

Greenhalgh, Trisha, 'Writing as therapy', *British Medical Journal 319*, pp 270–271, 1999

Henderson, Patti; Mascaro, Nathan; Rosen, David and Skillern, Tiffany; *The Healing Nature of Mandalas: Empirical Study of Active Imagination*, Texas AandM University, USA, 2005

McGuire, Beckwith, et al, 'Autonomic Effects of Expressive Writing in Individuals with Elevated Blood Pressure', *Journal of Health Psychology 10*, pp 197–209, 2005

SmithBattle, Lee, et al, 'Listening to the Baby: Evaluating a Baby Book Journal for New Parents', *Journal of Family Nursing 10*, pp 173–189, 2004

Smyth, Joshua M et al, 'Effects of Writing About Stressful Experiences on Symptom Reduction in Patients with Asthma or Rheumatoid Arthritis: A Randomised Trial', *JAMA – Journal of the American Medical Association*, 281 pp 1304–1309, 1999

Spiegel, John, 'Healing Words: Emotional Expression and Disease Outcome', *JAMA – Journal of the American Medical Association 282*, pp 1811–1812, 1999

Stanton, Annette L et al, 'Randomised Controlled Trial of Written Emotional Expression and Benefit Finding in Breast Cancer Patients', *Journal of Clinical Oncology*, 20:20 pp 4160–4168, 2002

Dealing with Terminal Illness
Sourby, Charles, Herbert H Lehman College, USA, 'The Relationship between Therapeutic Recreation and Palliation in the Treatment of the Advanced Cancer Patient', Website: *Therapeutic Recreation Directory*, http://www.recreationtherapy.com/cancer, accessed October 2005

Healing through Humour
Hughes, Clare, 'Medical Humour', editorial in *Student BMJ 11*, pp 308–309, 2003

Massam, Margaret and Moran, Carmen, 'An Evaluation of Humour in Emergency Work', *The Australasian Journal of Disaster and Trauma Studies*, 3, 1997

Mauger, Sylvia, 'The Use of Humour in Stress Management', International Stress Management Association, Stress News 13:3, 2001

Personal Growth
Bennett, D, 'Against Types', *Boston Globe USA*, 12 September 2004

Myers Briggs Type Indicator®, *The Myers and Briggs Foundation website* at http://www.myersbriggs.org/

Self-image
Leroy, Margaret, *Pleasure: The Truth about Female Sexuality*, HarperCollins, 1993

Index

Major page references are in **bold**

ABC technique **19–20**, 108–9, 168–9
achievements, celebrating 123
activating factors 101–2
addictions **98–104**, 188
alcoholism 99–100
alphabet and poetry 34
alternative medicine 41
anger
  and bereavement 46, 47, 52
  management **124–8**, 188
arts and therapy 10–11
artwork in journaling 29, 52, 165
auto-immune diseases 132–5

Bantu 34
beliefs 18, **19–20**, 154
  personal 137–8
  see also negative thoughts; thought
    processes
bereavement **45–53**, 187
  see also death; grief
blessings, counting 113
blogs 26, 186
boundary setting 99

career changes 158–162
change
  of job 158–162
  and loss 43–4
  of thought processes 11, 17
cheerfulness 135
childhood experiences
  abuse 99, **105–111**, 188
  and self-esteem 150
children
  death of **54–8**, 187
  health of 83–4
  and relationship breakdown 59–63
clustering **113–4**, 177
Cognitive Behaviour Therapy

(CBT) 7, 17
compulsive behaviour see addictions
conversations in writing 50
cost/benefit analysis 65, 101, 175
counselling see therapy
couple's journals 68

death 136–7
  of a child **54–8**, 187
  see also bereavement; grief
depression 18–9, **93–7**, 188
diaries 21
  in history 23, **24–7**
divorce see relationship breakdown

eating disorders 112–5, 188
emotional health 89–92, 187
emotions 42
equipment **28–30**, 187
expert practitioners 125
Expressive Arts Therapy 10–11

feelings
  exploring 16
  expressing in grief 45–6
  and job loss 76
  as metaphor 36
  and relationship breakdown 69–70
fight or flight reaction 117–8
food and emotional health 90–1, 114–5
Frank, Anne 25–6
friendship 77–81

goals and objective setting 17, 115,
  145–6, **163–4**
  and addictions 103
  and self-acceptance 155–6
grief 43–4
  stages of 45
  theories 174
  see also bereavement; death

habits, destructive 156–7
Haiku 37
headaches 121
healing 13–4, 41–2, 187
limitations of medicine 38–41
health 155
  emotional **89–92**, 187
  loss of 82–8
  physical **129**, 188–9
  spiritual 143–4
honesty 46–7
humour **140–2**, 189

illness 129–131
  diagnosis 132
  terminal 136–9
  see also health, loss of
inner child 110–11

jobs
  changing 158–162
  loss of 73–6
journaling 21–2
  benefits of 10, 11, 12, 14–5,
    17, 143–4
  and health 13–4
  history of 23–7
  and men 25
  prompts 165, 182
  and REBT 19–20
Jung, Carl 146

laughter 140–2
letter writing 96–7, 110, 134, 139
  to a child 61–2
  to a partner 70
lists
  making 133
  and poetry 35
loss 43–4, 48–9
  see also bereavement
loved ones
  grieving for 49–53
  illness of 86–8

marriage *see* relationship breakdown
medications **130–1**, 133, 180
medicine
  alternative 41
  limitations of 38–41
meditation 170–3
men 27
  diary writers 23
mental health 89
metaphor in poetry 36
mind mapping 113–4
miscarriage 55–7
moments in time, capturing 49
moods
  and food 90–1, 114
  spotting trends 102
Myers Briggs Type Indicator 146

negative
  self-talk 104
  thoughts 17, **18–9**, 94, **95–7**, 108,
    168–9
Neurolinguistic Programming 125

pain, remembering 147–8
paper 28–9
Pennebaker, James 93, 129, 130
pens 30
pentagrams 143
personal growth **145–9**, 163–4, 189
personality, examining 146–9
photographs **50–1**, 108
pillow books 24
pleasures 123
  remembering 148
poetry **33–7**, 47–8, 187
  and emotional health 89, 91–2
pregnancy 55–6
preserving journals 30–1
problems, understanding 101
project management 103

Rational emotive Behaviour Therapy
  (REBT) 7, **11–12**, **18–9**, 151

and journaling **19–20**, 108
and stress 119
realistic thinking 18
relationship breakdown 64, **69–72**, 187
    and children 59–63
    exercises to address problems 65–9
    see also friendship
relaxation 170–3
rewards 152–3
rhythm 33, 36

Sappho 23
self-esteem 71, **150–3**
self-image **154–7**, 189
self-knowledge 146–9
self-nurturing 152–3
senses and poetry 35
skills **31–2**, 187
SMART guidelines 103, 176
social readjustment rating scale 178–9
spiritual wellbeing 143–4
stillbirth 57–8
stream-of-consciousness writing 109
stress **116–123**, 178–9, 188
    symptoms 119–120, 121
SWOT analysis 181

talking therapies 7, 10, **16–20**, 186
terminal illness **136–9**, 189
therapy 10–12
thought processes
    changing 11, 17
    and healing 42
    negative 17, 18–9, 94, **95–7**, 108,
        168–9
    see also beliefs
transformation 85
trauma 39–40
trend spotting 102–3
triggers
    and addictive behaviour 101–3
    and anger 126–8
    and stress **116–9**, 122

weblogs 26, 186
work and change 158–162
writing
    ability 31–2
    and depression 93–94
    prompts for 165, 182
    to yourself 15, 152